M000230927

THE
BOUNTY
OF
ALLAH

COMPILED AND TRANSLATED BY
ANEELA KHALID ARSHED

THE
BOUNTY
OF
ALLAH

▲▲▲▲

Daily Reflections from
the Qur'an and
Islamic Traditions

A Crossroad Book
The Crossroad Publishing Company
New York

The Crossroad Publishing Company
370 Lexington Avenue, New York, NY 10017

Printed in the United States of America

Library of Congress Cataloging-in-Publication Data

Arshed, Aneela Khalid.
    The bounty of Allah : daily reflections from the Qur'an and
Islamic tradition / by Aneela Khalid Arshed.
        p.   cm.
    Includes bibliographical references.
    ISBN 0-8245-1823-3 (hc.)
    1. Koran–Theology. 2. Koran–Reading. 3. Koran–Study and
teaching. 4. Hadith–Criticism, interpretation, etc. 5. Sufism.
I. Title.
BP132.A77   1999
297.3′822–dc21   99–35104

1   2   3   4   5   6   7   8   9   10   04   03   02   01   00   99

FOR SABRINA AND DANNY

PREFACE

We live in a world filled with pain and suffering, and like all living creatures we have the need to be healed. Life on this planet is nothing short of a "dark night of the soul" within which we wander isolated and confused. Despite its advances modern medicine is still bewildered by the complexities of the human psyche. The phenomena of the psyche are deep and can be understood only when we turn inward and discover the numinous within. Though science and religion have frequently been at odds, few can deny the existence of a Higher Power, whose energy pulsates at the core of the universe. That same energy throbs inside each one of us, and once it is discovered, the dark world of shadows disappears, reawakening us to a new sense of well-being. Fear turns to hope, hope to faith, faith to knowledge, knowledge to understanding, and understanding to transformation.

I spent many years trying to understand my place in the universe: Where did I come from, where am I going, and what is my purpose in the world? Why is candor recompensed by deceit? Why does injustice dominate the world? Time and again I learned new lessons from my failures and found new answers to my questions. I began to see life from a different perspective. I discovered that adversity can lead to inner strength, patience to insight, and forgiveness to compassion, which is the threshold to freedom. All suffering has a purpose; if we are to heal, we must hold on to hope.

During my darkest times, I read the Qur'an for hours every day and highlighted each verse that helped me make sense of this non-sense world. It was a desperate attempt to overcome my fears, for like many of my fellow human beings, I had turned to God with my troubles and sought solace and fortitude to deal with my weaknesses. After years of austere discipline and ardent meditation, I came face to face with all my shortcomings and realized it was time to change, time to let go, time to forgive myself, and time to forgive everyone else. Though there were days when I thought I just could not go on, I managed somehow, living one day at a time, clinging to the belief that "this too shall pass."

I began to look beyond myself and realized that all human beings are looking for answers. Though a few have been endowed with inner vision, the majority of us are still lost within the chaos of our times. We yearn for comfort but are too constrained by time to pick up the Scripture and allow its puissant bounty to permeate our souls with much-needed peace.

With that in mind I selected short verses from the Qur'an and compiled a book of daily inspirations. I read several translations, both Urdu and English, and decided to base my undertaking on Pickthall's English translation (see the bibliography on p. 383), but I modified the English to suit modern readers. To further elucidate the deeper meaning of the text, I selected for each day words of the *hadith* (that is, the collective body of traditions relating to Muhammad and his companions) or citations from Sufi masters. I have indicated where many of these passages can be found in English translation, but most of the English translations here are based on my own consultation of the original Persian and Arabic sources as well as Urdu translations.

These selections were initially meant for myself alone, but I felt the need to share the inner peace that I acquired by meditating upon these verses over many years. As we read these verses day after day, we begin to reflect upon ourselves, upon what we have done, what we have left undone, and what we must accomplish in order to reach our goal. A new understanding begins to blossom within our beings, and our inner world begins to be transformed, very quietly, without our knowing it, until we feel God's healing touch deep within our hearts. In that moment our lives change forever. For the first time we realize how insignificant we really are, yet how special we must be to God. Then follows the awareness that sometimes in order to help us, He allows us to experience hardship. Slowly we learn to look upon the Lord as our Shepherd, who at times frightens, at others admonishes, yet always indulges His flock, reminding the lost sheep never to fret, for the doors of His forgiveness never close.

It is my hope that through this book readers may be comforted, just as I was, by the knowledge that He is near and listening to our secret pleas for help. May the essence of His Being enrich our lives with hope and peace.

✷

I am grateful to all the wonderful persons who took the time to help and encourage me in this monumental task, particularly the members of the Education Department of the Islamic Center of Long Island: Dr. Sultan Hameed, who initially guided me in the proper channels; Sana Nadeem and Jehan Ara Akbar, who shared their precious time and lent some priceless books to me; Ahmad Zenhom, a scholar and tutor of Islam and the Qur'an; Sabeeha Rehman of the Muslim Majlis of Staten Island, who took the time to read the manuscript; Dr. Asma Ejaz and Leah Shinbach, who enlightened me about the medical aspects of prayer and meditation; Mr. and Mrs. Ehsan Khan, who lent me a treasury of supplications; and Mr. and Mrs. Ahmad Khan, who provided much appreciated emotional support. Most of all I want to thank my wonderful husband, without whose tender support this would have been an exceptionally difficult project.

I could never have completed this book without the guidance of my father, A. K. Khalid, a renowned scholar and a master of Eastern languages.

JANUARY

JANUARY 1

In the name of Allah,
the Most Gracious and Merciful.
Praise be to You, O Lord of the worlds,
the Beneficent, the Merciful.
Master of the day of Justice,
You alone we worship,
to You alone we appeal for help.
Show us the straight path,
the path of those You blessed,
not the path of those You condemned,
nor of those who go astray.

THE OPENING 1:1–7

*He that follows the path of knowledge shall
find Allah easing the path to Paradise for him.*

The Prophet Muhammad, as reported by
Anas bin Malik, *Al-Hadis,* 1:351[1]

JANUARY 2

Humankind! Worship your Lord who created you and those before you that you may remain conscious of Him.

THE COW[2] 2:21

The Merciful is kind to those who are merciful. If you show compassion to your fellow creatures in this world, then those in heaven shall be compassionate toward you.

The Prophet Muhammad, as reported by Abd'Allah bin Amr, *Al-Hadis,* 1:339

January 3

We said, all of you descend from here [Paradise]; and there [on earth] you shall be guided by Us. Then those who follow Our commandments shall have nothing to fear, nor shall they grieve.

THE COW 2:38

If you have no eyes, do not walk blindly;
take a staff in your hand.
If you have no staff of insight,
do not walk without a guide.

Rumi, *Mathnawi,* 3:276–78

JANUARY 4

Establish worship, give in alms, and bow your heads with those who bow down in worship.

THE COW 2:43

Those who content themselves with limited provender, submitting themselves before Allah's will, shall find even a few good deeds of theirs sufficient for divine approval.

The Prophet Muhammad, as reported by
'Ali bin Abi Talib, *Al-Hadis,* 1:279

JANUARY 5

Seek comfort in patience and prayer; indeed it is difficult, but not for the devout, who know that they will meet their Lord and that to Him they shall return.

THE COW 2:45–46

Hidden creatures good and bad always touch the heart. The touch of the angel is inspiration; Satanic touches temptations untold. Tarry with patience until your confusion is resolved and you know whom you rejected and who became the leader of your heart.

Rumi, *Mathnawi*, 1:1035, 1038–39

JANUARY 6

Those who believe and remain righteous are destined for Paradise, and therein shall they abide.

THE COW 2:82

Real faith is having complete trust in God. "It is the belief in the wisdom which comes from the Unseen." Such certainty can only be attained through the knowledge that emerges with divine help.

Al-Hujwiri, *The Kashf al-Mahjub*, p. 290

January 7

The Lord shall reward those who surrender
their purpose to Him and remain steadfast;
neither fear nor grief shall overcome them.

THE COW 2:112

*Surrender yourselves before God in the manner
of the devout saints; then God will hold you
just as dearly as He did the devout who went
before you. Therefore follow His commandments and bear every affliction with patience.
Adhere consciously for this was the path chosen by the sages, the path that will lead you to
the ultimate freedom.*

Sheikh Abdul Qadir Jillani,
Fayuz E Yazdani, p. 23

January 8

To Allah belong the East and the West. Wherever you turn your face, there is the countenance
of the Lord. Behold! Allah is All-Embracing,
All-Cognizant.

THE COW 2:115

As he beheld the light of God he felt protected,
and was delivered from the throes of doubt.

Rumi, *Mathnawi,* 5:2451

JANUARY 9

As Abraham and Ishmael raised the foundations of the House[3] (Abraham) adjured, "Lord! Accept this homage from us. You, only You are the All-Encompassing, All-Cognizant. Our Lord, allow us to surrender ourselves to You and from our offspring a nation that will be submissive to You. Enlighten us with our ways of worship and relent toward us. Lord, You alone are the Most Relenting, the Most Compassionate."

THE COW 2:127–28

A true Muslim is the one who does not defame or abuse others; but the truly righteous becomes a refuge for humankind, their lives and their properties.

The Prophet Muhammad, as reported by
Abd'Allah bin Amr, Al-Hadis, 1:123

JANUARY 10

Who save the foolish would forsake the religion of Abraham? Indeed he was Our chosen servant in this world, and in the hereafter he shall dwell among the virtuous. When his Lord said to him, "Surrender yourself to Me!" he answered, "I have surrendered myself to the Lord of the worlds."

THE COW 2:130–31

My Lord, how great my desire to meet You, how earnest my hope of Your reward. O Most Gracious, Hope of all hope, O Adored by all, if I be unworthy of You, and my endeavors not deserving of devotion, then gladly shall I confess to my infirmities, my sins. For who could be more forgiving than Yourself? But should You choose to chastise me, I will satisfy myself in the knowledge that no one could be more just than You.

Sha'wana, in Rabi'a the Mystic, p. 147

JANUARY 11

We observe you as you turn your face toward the heaven seeking guidance. We enjoin
you now to turn in prayer toward the Qibla.[4]
Therefore turn your face toward the inviolable
House of Worship. And all of you, wherever
you may be, turn your faces toward it. Behold those who have received the Scriptures
know that this revelation is the Truth. Allah is
cognizant of what they do.

THE COW 2:144

*If you devote yourself to God in this world, He
will admit you among His chosen servants in
the hereafter. Such devotion, however, demands
sacrifice and self-denial, the two instruments
that make union with God possible.*

Al-Hujwiri, *The Kashf al-Mahjub*, p. 201

JANUARY 12

Every community has a direction toward which it turns for worship, so strive hard and pursue illustrious endeavors. In the end Allah will bring you all together wherever you may be. Behold Allah has the power to ordain anything.

THE COW 2:148

Every community hallows a special place
through which it might transcend one day.
Kind delights in kind,
so delight in the observance,
but follow the way of perfection
or you may adhere to the "Other."

Rumi, *Mathnawi*, 1:888–90

JANUARY 13

Remember Me, and I will remember you. Be grateful to Me, and do not deny My favors.

THE COW 2:152

The devil reposes in the hearts of the children of Adam. When they remember Allah, he retracts; when heedless he whispers evil therein.

The Prophet Muhammad, as reported by
Abd'Allah ibn Abbas, *Al-Hadis,* 3:732

January 14

O you who believe! Strengthen yourselves with resolution and prayer. Indeed Allah is with those who persevere in adversity.

THE COW 2:153

Do not lose hope in adversity and complain that God singled you out for punishment, remitting others guilty of worse sins. Your present state could very well be His intent to elevate your spiritual station; or He could just be testing your faith. Every day that you persevere, you grow closer to perfection. Thus your present despair may be the beginning of an infinite blessing.

Sheikh Abdul Qadir Jillani,
Futhul Ghaib, pp. 70, 71

January 15

We shall test your faith by means of fear and hunger and loss of wealth and lives and crops, but give good tidings to those who endured with courage, who in hardship say, "To Allah we belong and to Him shall we return."

The Cow 2:155–56

If you are destined for good fortune you will be blessed; if afflictions have been ordained, no matter where you hide they will seek you out. Submit therefore before the will of God; be grateful in well-being and endure adversity with fortitude that His light may radiate within your being.

Sheikh Abdul Qadir Jillani,
Futhul Ghaib, p. 43.

JANUARY 16

Your God is one God! There is no God save Him, the Beneficent, the Merciful. Behold, in the creation of the heavens and the earth, the interchange of the night and the day, the ships that set sail with cargo, the rainfall that showers from the sky reviving the earth after its death causing all living things to proliferate therein, in the regulation of the winds and the clouds that remain suspended between the heaven and the earth, there are signs of Allah's sovereignty for the discerning.

THE COW 2:163–64

O Merciful Lord, help us live in harmony with each other. Grant us forbearance that we may see the way. Deliver us from the darkness (of hate) and show us the light. Elevate our state and guide us on Your way.

Cited in the collection
Munajat E Maqbool, p. 83

JANUARY 17

O you who believe! Partake of the good things
that We have provided for you, and render
thanks to Allah if it is He whom you worship.

THE COW 2:172

*We cannot do away with our daily nourish-
ment, but let us not wallow in gluttony. Abu
Yazid was once asked why he regarded fasting so supreme. He replied, "Had the Pharaoh
known hunger he would not have declared
himself God. And Korah would never have
been so rebellious had he endured the pain of
starvation."*

Al-Hujwiri, *The Kashf al-Mahjub*, p. 347

JANUARY 18

O you who believe! Fasting is ordained for you, as it was ordained for those before you, that you may attain piety. Fast a certain number of days, but those among you who are sick or traveling may fast the same number of days at a later time. But for those who are able to fast and do not, there is still redemption in the feeding of a needy person. However, for those who are given to increased virtue on their own accord, it is more valuable for them, though fasting is far better for you, if only you knew.

THE COW 2:183–84

Abstinence is better than seeking a remedy.
Scratching the abrasion only makes it worse.
Fasting is the foremost principle of medicine.
Fast, and behold the strength of the spirit.

Rumi, *Mathnawi*, 1:2910–11

JANUARY 19

Spend your wealth in the way of Allah, and do not by your own hands cast yourselves to ruin. Grow in goodness, for Allah loves the beneficent.

THE COW 2:195

Do not be confused by ignorance; turn toward and not away from Allah. Have faith in Him and refrain from transgression. For it is Allah and no other creature who can grant or take away life. He is the Infinite and will always reign Supreme. He bestows prosperity, and decrees poverty. Fear Him alone and none other; adhere to Him that you may prevail.

Sheikh Abdul Qadir Jillani,
Fayuz E Yazdani, p. 74

January 20

Among them are those who adjure, "Our Lord! Bestow upon us in this world that which is worthy and also in the hereafter that which is superlative, and save us from the doom of the Fire."

The Cow 2:201

Allah says, "I am with My servant when he remembers Me and his lips move in My service."

The Prophet Muhammad, as reported by Abu Hurairah, *Al-Hadis*, 3:732

JANUARY 21

Those who believe and those who forsake their homelands for the fear of persecution and strive hard in the way of Allah shall be blessed by His mercy. Verily Allah is the Most Forgiving and Most Merciful.

THE COW 2:218

He turned toward the heaven and said,
"Answer the prayers of Your pilgrims.
O You who bestow all blessings on me,
I seek my sustenance only from You."
In the midst of his litany a cloud appeared
and began to pour rain that settled in a basin.
The miracle elevated one group,
their faith now certainty that God knows best.

Rumi, *Mathnawi*, 2:3802–3, 3805–6, 3808

JANUARY 22

Who will offer to Allah a goodly loan, that He may amply repay, multiplying it manifold? For it is He who takes away and He who rewards abundantly and to Him shall you all return.

THE COW 2:245

Hasten with your charity, because disaster does not trample it.

The Prophet Muhammad, as reported by 'Ali bin Abi Talib, *Al-Hadis,* 2:22

JANUARY 23

Allah! There is no God save Him, the Living, the Eternal. Neither slumber nor sleep overtakes Him. To Him belongs all that is in the heavens and on the earth. Who can intercede with Him save by His leave? He knows all that lies before human beings and what remains hidden from them, and He permits them to comprehend only that knowledge which He determines. His infinite Throne overspreads the heavens and the earth, and He is never fatigued or tired of protecting them. Only He is the truly Exalted, the Tremendous.

THE COW 2:255

Give up deception and take heed. You say you fear Allah; in truth you fear his creatures. Fear neither jinn,[5] nor humans, nor angels. Fear not the beast, nor the scourge of this world, or the hereafter. Fear only the Creator, the Sovereign who created all.

Sheikh Abdul Qadir Jillani,
Fayuz E Yazdani, p. 158

JANUARY 24

Those who spend their wealth in the way of
Allah and do not follow their benevolence by
reproach and harsh words shall find their reward with the Lord. They shall neither be
overcome by fear nor shall they grieve.

THE COW 2:262

*The best charity is followed by contentment so
begin with those related to you.*

The Prophet Muhammad, as reported by
Abu Hurairah, *Al-Hadis,* 2:21

JANUARY 25

A Kind word with forgiveness is preferred over charity followed by injury. Allah is Absolute, Clement.

THE COW 2:263

Beware of the pleas of the oppressed, because they will ask for justice from Allah, and Allah does not deny the rights of the deserving.

The Prophet Muhammad, as reported by 'Ali bin Abi Talib, *Al-Hadis,* 1:340

JANUARY 26

He bestows wisdom on whom He will, and those who receive the gift of wisdom have indeed been blessed with an abundant wealth. But no one save the prudent remember that.

THE COW 2:269

It is amazing how people overlook the blessings bestowed upon them by the grace of God and covet what the wealthy enjoy. Had they observed those inferior to them, they would have seen the wonderful gifts with which God blessed them. More amazing is the fact that they notice those inferior to them in religion but seldom those who are better than themselves.

Al-Ghazzali, *Ihya Ulum Id-Din,* 4:116

JANUARY 27

It is noble if you make your charity public, but
far superior is the charity that helps the needy
in secret; it will atone for some of your sins.
Allah is indeed cognizant of all that you do.

THE COW 2:271

*Fools exult in life while the pious prepare for
the journey ahead. A major portion of their
wealth is spent in God's way, and they themselves suffice with the bare minimum, striving
toward the hereafter. They even sacrifice fine
victuals confident in the faith that they shall be
blessed with better in the hereafter. Even God
cherishes them because of their conviction and
devotion.*

Sheikh Abdul Qadir Jillani,
Fayuz E Yazdani, p. 96

JANUARY 28

Lord! Do not cause our hearts to go astray after You have guided us on the right path. Bestow upon us the gift of Your divine benevolence. You alone can confer true Grace.

THE FAMILY OF 'IMRAN 3:8

If you adhere to the things that I am leaving behind, you shall never be misguided.

The Prophet Muhammad, as reported by Ja'bir bin Abd'Allah, *Al-Hadis*, 1:172

JANUARY 29

Allah sees all that is in the hearts of His servants, those who say, "Our Lord! We believe in You, forgive us our sins and save us from the doom of the Fire," those who are steadfast, truthful, and devout, who give in charity and pray for forgiveness in the depths of the night.

THE FAMILY OF 'IMRAN 3:15–17

Allah loves those who sacrifice their repose and arise in the depths of the night to glorify the word of their Lord; those who give in charity without making their identity public; and those who uphold their ranks even when their companions have been overcome.

The Prophet Muhammad, as reported by
Abd'Allah bin Mas'ud, *Al-Hadis*, 2:18

JANUARY 30

Allah Himself bears witness that there is no
God but Him. The angels and those endowed
with wisdom also bear witness that there is no
God save Him. Only He executes true justice;
indeed He is the Omnipotent, Judicious.

THE FAMILY OF 'IMRAN 3:18

*Once the ego is overcome peace follows. "Only
God and no living creature has the power to
control destinies." With that conviction entrust
all your cares to the Lord and follow the path
of the Truth, conforming to the divine edicts,
until you attain union with Him and become
as pure as Adam before whom all creatures
prostrated.*

Sheikh Abdul Qadir Jillani,
Fayuz E Yazdani, p. 341

JANUARY 31

Say,[6] "Allah, O King of all kings! You bestow
sovereignty to whom You will, and You withdraw sovereignty from whom You will. You
exalt whom You will, and You abase whom
You will. In Your hand lies all that is worthy.
You have power over all things."

THE FAMILY OF 'IMRAN 3:26

*God bestows good fortune on whom He will.
Then why do you feel jealous and wish that another be dispossessed of all his prosperity? Do
you know in your wrath you deem yourselves
equal to God? Behold, you will be depraved,
because envy corrodes faith and leads to the ultimate fall. Bear in mind Joseph, who despite
his brothers' loathsome schemes, remained the
illustrious. And who but the brothers were disgraced? Take heed, time and again our Lord
warns us against the ills of envy.*

Sheikh Abdul Qadir Jillani,
Futhul Ghaib, pp. 103–4

FEBRUARY

FEBRUARY 1

Say, "If you love Allah then follow me. Allah will love you and forgive you your sins. For Allah is the Most Benevolent, the Most Merciful."

THE FAMILY OF 'IMRAN 3:31

Eat what you want and dress up as you desire, as long as extravagance and pride do not mislead you.

The Prophet Muhammad, as reported by Abd'Allah ibn Abbas, *Al-Hadis,* 1:645

FEBRUARY 2

Without doubt, Allah is my Lord and your
Lord, so worship Him, for that is the straight
path. But when Jesus became aware of their dis-
belief, he cried, "Who shall be my helpers in the
cause of Allah?"

And the disciples replied, "We shall be the
helpers of Allah. We believe in Him and bear
witness that we have surrendered ourselves before Him."

THE FAMILY OF 'IMRAN 3:51–52

The Jesus of your spirit lies within you:
ask for his help, for he is a great helper.
Do not seek of this Jesus delights of the body.
Do not ask your Moses the wish of a Pharaoh.
Do not be aggrieved by thoughts of sustenance;
you will be sustained.
Instead be steadfast
and frequent the divine court.

Rumi, *Mathnawi*, 2:450, 453–54

FEBRUARY 3

Our Lord! We believe in that which You have
revealed and we follow the apostle. Count us
among those who bear witness to the truth.

THE FAMILY OF 'IMRAN 3:53

*God fills the hearts of those who love Him
with peace, thus enabling them to endure afflictions with ease. And they also plead, "We
shall bear every torment (of this world) with
joy, but never shall we be able to endure being
separated from You. When Your magnificence
illumines our hearts, all our pain, our sorrows
seem meaningless and vanish."*

Al-Hujwiri, *The Kashf al-Mahjub*, p. 111

FEBRUARY 4

You shall not attain devoutness until you give in alms a portion of that which you cherish. Remember Allah is aware of all that you give in alms.

THE FAMILY OF 'IMRAN 3:92

Spend in the name of Allah and do not hold back lest Allah withhold His blessings from you.

The Prophet Muhammad, as reported by Asma bint Abu Bakr al-Saddiq, *Al-Hadis*, 2:24

FEBRUARY 5

Stay united and adhere to the faith of Allah, and let nothing sow dissension among you. Remember how He bestowed His favor upon you and united your hearts after your animosities that you became as brothers by His grace. You were upon the brink of the abyss of fire, yet He saved you from it. Thus Allah makes clear His revelations to You, that you may be guided.

THE FAMILY OF 'IMRAN 3:103

Renewing peace between two aggrieved parties surpasses ritual praying, fasting, and almsgiving.

The Prophet Muhammad, as reported by
Abu Darda'a, *Al-Hadis*, 1:325–26

FEBRUARY 6

There may spring from you a community that will invite to goodness, enjoining what is right and forbidding what is wrong. Such people shall certainly triumph.

THE FAMILY OF 'IMRAN 3:104

The most upright among you are those who carry themselves with the finest conduct.

The Prophet Muhammad, as reported by Abd'Allah bin Amr, *Al-Hadis,* 1:388

FEBRUARY 7

Whatever good they do, they shall not be denied the reward thereof. Allah is aware of those who attain to piety.

THE FAMILY OF 'IMRAN 3:115

Those who look after widows and the destitute are equal to the ones striving in the way of Allah and, in my eyes, the same as those who worship all night and fast all day.

The Prophet Muhammad, as reported by Abu Hurairah, *Al-Hadis*, 1:263

FEBRUARY 8

If you stay patient in adversity and restrain yourselves from evil, your Lord will help you with five thousand distinctively marked angels, should your enemy suddenly fall upon you. Allah ordained this as a message of hope for you, so that your hearts may find comfort, since victory comes only from Allah, the Almighty and the Wise.

THE FAMILY OF 'IMRAN 3:125–26

Allah tries his chosen people through many hardships, but those who persevere through adversity, surrendering themselves before the will of Allah, shall be blessed with a superb reward.

The Prophet Muhammad, as reported by
Anas bin Malik, *Al-Hadis*, 1:315

FEBRUARY 9

Vie with one another for forgiveness from your
Lord and for a Paradise as vast as the heavens
and the earth, prepared for those who fend off
evil, for those who spend (in His way) in comfort and in hardship, who control their anger
and forgive their fellow beings simply because
Allah loves the charitable; and if they ever commit evil, or wrong their souls, they remember
Allah and implore forgiveness for their sins,
for who save Allah can forgive, and do not
knowingly persist in wrongdoing.

THE FAMILY OF 'IMRAN 3:133–35

*A person who overcomes others by physical
strength is not powerful; the truly powerful are
those who control their wrath when aroused
to anger.*

The Prophet Muhammad, as reported by
Abu Hurairah, *Sahih al-Bukhari*, p. 962

FEBRUARY 10

Do not lose heart, nor fall into despair, for you shall gain the upper hand if you are indeed true in faith.

THE FAMILY OF 'IMRAN 3:139

Lord, bestow upon us that which is good in this world and that which is good in the life to come, and save us from the doom of the Fire.

The Prophet Muhammad, as reported by Anas bin Malik, *Sahih al-Bukhari,* p. 977 (2084)

FEBRUARY 11

No soul can die except by Allah's leave, for the term of every life is preordained. Those who desire the reward of this world shall be granted thereof; and those who desire the reward of the hereafter shall also be granted thereof. We shall indeed reward the grateful.

THE FAMILY OF 'IMRAN 3:145

If you wish to shine like the daylight, burn up the night of self-importance. Dissolve the self like copper in the elixir; dissolve in Him who fosters all existence. But you are bound by the discord of "I" and "We." The cause of your ruin is this sad dualism.

Rumi, *Mathnawi*, 1:3010–12

FEBRUARY 12

So Allah gave them the reward of this world and a magnificent reward of the hereafter. Allah loves those who excel in good deeds.

THE FAMILY OF 'IMRAN 3:148

A true believer loves for his brother what he loves for himself.

The Prophet Muhammad, as reported by Anas bin Malik, *Al-Hadis,* 1:113

FEBRUARY 13

Allah is your Protector; sufficient is He, the greatest of helpers.

THE FAMILY OF 'IMRAN 3:150

Lord! I seek refuge in You
from adversities, weaknesses, indolence,
cowardice, avarice, indebtedness,
and being victimized by the populace.

The Prophet Muhammad, as reported by
Anas bin Malik, *Al-Hadis,* 3:789

FEBRUARY 14

If Allah is your protector, none can overcome you, and if He forsakes you, then who can help you? Trust Allah and have faith in His sovereign power.

THE FAMILY OF 'IMRAN 3:160

I once saw a Christian monk gaunt through self-sacrifice and doubled over by the fear of God. I asked him to show me the path of God. He replied, "If you knew God you would know the way to Him. I worship Him although I do not know Him; you disobey Him though you know Him. With knowledge comes fear, yet you are self-assured; with heresy ignorance, yet I feel fear within me." His words moved me so deeply that since then I have refrained from wrongdoing.

Abd'Allah bin Mubarak al-Marwazi,
The Kashf al-Mahjub, p. 96

FEBRUARY 15

Indeed, Allah bestowed His grace upon the believers by sending them a Prophet of their own, who recited before them the Lord's revelations in order to purify and enlighten them through divine wisdom. For before that they were lost in grave error.

THE FAMILY OF 'IMRAN 3:164

Be it the world or the space He is with you. He chastises to make the impure pure. Neglect devotion and be bound by fetters of pain and doubt. Seek freedom, the remedy of all pain. Seek the roots from which sprout leaves and fruit. Water the roots and grow to perfection. And when the fruit blossoms, give it to your friends.

Rumi, *Mathnawi*, 3:346, 351–52, 362–63

FEBRUARY 16

Jubilant are they [the martyrs] because of the grace Allah bestowed upon them, rejoicing in the glad tidings given to those who were left behind and have not yet joined them, that they need have no fear, neither shall they grieve.

THE FAMILY OF 'IMRAN 3:170

Happy the man who freed himself from his "self" and united himself with the Infinite. When you sought refuge in the Qur'an of God, you mingled yourself with the essence of the prophets. The Qur'an is a narrative of the states of the prophets who glory in the blessed ocean of His majesty.

Rumi, *Mathnawi,* 1:1535, 1537–38

FEBRUARY 17

So they returned with grace and bounty from
Allah, and no harm touched them. For they
had striven to please Allah. Indeed Allah is of
infinite bounty.

THE FAMILY OF 'IMRAN 3:174

*Allah is compassionate and loves compassion in
all things.*

The Prophet Muhammad, as reported by
A'ishah bint Abi Bakr, *Al-Hadis*, 1:332

FEBRUARY 18

The kingdom of the heavens and the earth belongs to Allah. He indeed is able to do all things.

THE FAMILY OF 'IMRAN 3:189

Before He created life, the Almighty Allah declared, "My Mercy shall surpass My Wrath." Thus was it written.

The Prophet Muhammad, as reported by
Abu Hurairah, *Sahih al-Bukhari*,
p. 641 (1351)

FEBRUARY 19

Behold! In the creation of the heavens and the
earth and the alternation of the night and the
day are signs for people of understanding, those
who remember Allah as they stand and sit, and
lie down to rest, who reflect on the creation of
the heavens and the earth, and say, "Lord, You
did not create this in vain, glory be to You, save
us from the doom of the Fire."

THE FAMILY OF 'IMRAN 3:190–91

*I asked the Prophet to guide me with a supplication with which I could beseech Allah after
every prayer. He replied, "O Allah, I have done
great wrong to my soul and only You can absolve me of my sins. O Most Compassionate,
have mercy on me."*

Reported by Abu Bakr al-Saddiq,
Al-Hadis, 3:302

FEBRUARY 20

Lord! We heard a voice inviting us to faith, saying, "Believe in your Lord," and we believed.
O Sustainer, absolve us of our sins, remit from
us our evil deeds, and allow us to pass away as
the devout.

THE FAMILY OF 'IMRAN 3:193

*When a person wakes up in the early hours of
dawn, an angel proclaims, "Glorify the Lord,
Most Holy!"*

The Prophet Muhammad, as reported by
Al-Zubayr bin al-Awwam,
Al-Hadis, 3:743

FEBRUARY 21

Those who remain righteous shall abide forever in gardens embellished by flowing streams
as a welcoming reward from their Lord. And
that which Allah has in store for the upright is
positively magnificent.

THE FAMILY OF 'IMRAN 3:198

Good conjecture is a gift from divine grace.

The Prophet Muhammad, as reported by
Abu Hurairah, *Al-Hadis,* 1:552

FEBRUARY 22

O you who believe! Endure, outdo all others in endurance, encourage each other, and observe your obligation to Allah that you may succeed.

THE FAMILY OF 'IMRAN 3:200

Wisdom and power follow endurance and patience.

The Prophet Muhammad, as reported by Abu Sayeed al-Khodri, *Al-Hadis,* 1:442

FEBRUARY 23

Allah forgives those who commit evil in ignorance but quickly turn to Him in repentance. Such persons shall find Allah compassionate. Allah is full of knowledge and wisdom.

WOMEN 4:17

God calls Himself "Baseer" [Observant], so that the knowledge that He is watching you may keep you from sinning.

Rumi, *The Life and Thought of Rumi*, p. 75

FEBRUARY 24

Allah wishes to explain to you and guide you
by the examples of those who lived before you
and to turn to you in compassion. Allah is
Cognizant, Wise.

WOMEN 4:26

I heard the Prophet narrate the story of another
Prophet [Jesus] before him, whose people beat
him and caused him to bleed. Even as he wiped
the blood off his face he said, "Lord, forgive
them for they know not what they do!"

Reported by Nayeem bin Mas'ud,
Sahih al-Bukhari, p. 687

February 25

Allah wishes to lighten your burdens, for man was created weak.

WOMEN 4:28

His words were filled with such eloquence and wisdom, as though an ocean abided inside him, and the ocean filled with eloquent pearls. The light that shone from every pearl became a criterion of right and wrong.

Rumi, *Mathnawi*, 2:849–51

FEBRUARY 26

If you abstain from those major sins that have been forbidden upon you, We shall remit from you your minor evils and shall admit you into an eternal abode of glory.

Women 4:31

This religion is easy. Do not make it a rigor, or you shall be overcome. Be steadfast, seek the closeness of Allah, grow in virtue, and implore His appeasement day and night.

The Prophet Muhammad, as reported by
Abu Hurairah, *Al-Hadis*, 1:431

February 27

Allah does not wrong anyone in the least. If there is a good deed, He will double it and will confer from His own grace an immense reward.

WOMEN 4:40

The visions now revealed to you,
once they seemed absurd to you.
From ten prisons His bounty released you.
Make not the desert a prison for you.

Rumi, *Mathnawi*, 3:3656–57

FEBRUARY 28

Allah has full knowledge of your enemies. Sufficient is He as your Protector, and sufficient is He to comfort you.

WOMEN 4:45

A believer shall not be stung twice out of the same hole.[7]

The Prophet Muhammad, as reported by Abu Hurairah, *Al-Hadis,* 1:126

FEBRUARY 29

Have you seen those who consider themselves pure? Allah alone purifies whom He will. No one shall be wronged in the least.

WOMEN 4:49

Do not be ruled by lust; seek freedom by following the righteous. Mere claims of piety will not earn you inner freedom. Remain patient in adversity to attain peace, for adversity is the threshold to freedom. Those who cannot persevere are held back from the doors of Mercy.

Sheikh Abdul Qadir Jillani,
Fayuz E Yazdani, p. 262

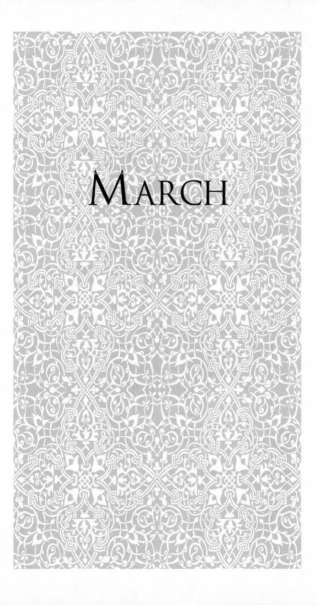

MARCH

MARCH 1

Those who obey Allah and His messenger shall
reside among those upon whom the Lord bestowed His divine approval. These are the
prophets, the saints, the martyrs, and the
righteous. What a delightful company shall
they be.

WOMEN 4:69

Day and night he danced in ecstasy,
revolving on the earth like the heavens.
His ecstatic cries reached the zenith of the skies
and were heard by all and sundry.

Rumi, *The Life and Thought*
of Rumi, p. 104

March 2

When you are greeted by someone, let your greeting be better than theirs or at least return the greeting. Allah keeps count of all things.

WOMEN 4:86

The best of the people are the first to greet others.

The Prophet Muhammad, as reported by Abu Umamah, *Al-Hadis,* 1:571

MARCH 3

Turn to Allah and implore forgiveness. For indeed Allah is Most Forgiving and Merciful.

WOMEN 4:106

Worship the Merciful, feed the hungry, and spread peace. You shall then enter Paradise in peace.

The Prophet Muhammad, as reported by Abd'Allah bin Amr, *Al-Hadis*, 2:15

MARCH 4

He who transgresses or wrongs his own soul
but then turns to Allah seeking forgiveness shall
find Allah Forgiving, Merciful.

WOMEN 4:110

When temptation claims your reason,
know that misfortune is about to strike.
Fall down prostrate and begin to pray.
With flowing tears implore the Lord
that He may deliver you
from the throes of doubt.

Rumi, *Mathnawi*, 4:385–86

MARCH 5

Those who render good deeds, be they male or female, and believe in the Almighty shall enter Paradise. They will not be wronged by the least injustice.

WOMEN 4:124

A believer through his good deeds reaches the position of one who worships all night and fasts during the day.

The Prophet Muhammad, as reported by A'ishah bint Abi Bakr, *Al-Hadis*, 1:388

MARCH 6

Who is loftier in religion than those who surrender themselves before Allah's will and remain virtuous, following the faith of Abraham the upright? Allah Himself chose Abraham for a friend.

WOMEN 4:125

Sever the chains of the ego. Set yourself free and witness the bright essence of your inner being. Discover within your heart the wisdom of a prophet without books, without teachers, and without prudence.

Rumi, *The Life and Thought of Rumi*, p. 169

MARCH 7

All that lies between the heavens and the earth belongs to Allah. Allah encompasses all things.

WOMEN 4:126

Since the dawn of human consciousness, religion has been the mightiest force driving humankind toward an unknown goal. It has allowed the teeming millions to experience a greater joy and a creative fervor; it has furnished them with the strength and the courage to achieve imperishable cultural feats and enabled them to reach unimaginable spiritual heights.

Muhammad Asad Leopold Weiss,
in *Islamic Sufism*, p. 8

MARCH 8

Believers, remain resolute in justice and bear witness to the truth, be it against yourselves, your parents, or your kinsfolk. Whether the person concerned is rich or poor, remember that Allah is cognizant of your actions. So do not let your passions take control, lest you swerve from justice. For if you distort the truth or decline to give your testimony, then remember Allah has full knowledge of all that you do.

WOMEN 4:135

He wept when they appointed him judge. The deputy asked, "Why do cry? This is the time to rejoice."

"How can I who does not know decide between two who know?"

"Accept no bribe," the deputy said. "Then you will know. Do not give in to desire; it will make you blind. Since I turned from vain desires, my heart has become like a mirror bright. It recognizes truth from untruth."

Rumi, *Mathnawi*, 2:2744–46, 2753–55

MARCH 9

Allah does not favor the utterance of harsh speech, save by those who have been truly wronged. Indeed Allah hears all, knows all.

WOMEN 4:148

Fear oppression, because oppression will be intense darkness on the Day of Resurrection.

The Prophet Muhammad, as reported by Ibn Umar, *Al-Hadis,* 1:333

MARCH 10

Whether you remain worthy openly or in secret or forgive an injustice against you, know that Allah is the Most Clement, Powerful.

WOMEN 4:149

Fear Allah wherever you may be, and repel evil with goodness, for that will efface all its negative results.

The Prophet Muhammad, as reported by Abu Dharr, *Al-Hadis,* 1:388–89

MARCH 11

Allah shall certainly reward those who believe
in their Lord and all His messengers and do not
make any distinction between them. Allah is the
Most Compassionate, the Merciful.

WOMEN 4:152

The stories of the prophets in the Qur'an sad-
den the soul within its prison. The captive soul
seeks freedom from ignorance. Look to the
prophets, those souls freed from bonds. Their
voices call from within their religions, "This is
the way! Escape! Escape! This is the way we
escaped. There is no other way but our way."

Rumi, *Mathnawi,* 1:1540–44

MARCH 12

Humankind, you have received manifest proof from your Lord. A radiant light to dispel your darkness was sent down to you. Those who believe in their Lord and hold fast to Him shall be admitted to His grace and bounty. He will guide them to Himself by the straight path.

WOMEN 4:175–76

Once a person asked the Prophet, "What is true faith?"

The Prophet replied, "When your good endeavors bring you pleasure and your transgressions cause you anguish, you know that you are a person of faith."

Reported by Abu Umamah,
Al-Hadis, 1:115

MARCH 13

Remember the grace that Allah bestowed upon you and the covenant by which He bound you when you said, "We hear and we obey." So keep your duty to Allah. Allah is aware of all that you hide in your hearts.

THE TABLE SPREAD 5:7

Your will be done, my Lord, my Messiah!
Your will be done, my desire, my aspiration!
O essence of my being, my goal, my religion!
O all of my all, my hearing, my sight!

Al-Hallaj, Mansur,
The Kashf al-Mahjub, p. 259

MARCH 14

Allah has promised forgiveness and an immense reward to those who believe and remain righteous.

THE TABLE SPREAD 5:9

Those who show compassion to the weak, treat parents gently, and pardon the enslaved shall be granted an easy death and the delights of Paradise.

The Prophet Muhammad, as reported by Ja'bir bin Abd'Allah, *Al-Hadis,* 1:187

MARCH 15

Believers, do not forget how Allah bestowed His favor upon you by restraining the hands of those who sought to harm you; so remain conscious of Allah, and depend only upon your Lord.

THE TABLE SPREAD 5:11

If you are dependable, honest, virtuous, and content in Allah's will, no harm shall come your way.

The Prophet Muhammad, as reported by Abd'Allah bin Amr, *Al-Hadis,* 1:475

MARCH 16

Believers, remain conscious of Allah and seek the path that leads to Him. Strive in His way that you may prosper.

THE TABLE SPREAD 5:35

If you wish for light, be ready to receive light.
Nourish your ego and be deprived of light.
If you wish to find a way out of this prison,
do not turn away;
bow down in worship and draw near.

Rumi, *Mathnawi*, 1:3606–7

MARCH 17

Believers, be they Jewish, Sabean,[8] or Christian — all those who believe in the Omnipotent and the Last Day and remain righteous — shall have nothing to fear nor shall they grieve.

THE TABLE SPREAD 5:69

I am neither Christian, nor Jewish, nor Muslim. Doing away with duality, I saw the two worlds as one. I seek One, I know One, I see One, and I call One.

Rumi, *The Life and Thought of Rumi*, p. 118

MARCH 18

When they listen to the revelation received by
the messenger, you see their eyes fill with tears
because of their recognition of the Truth. And
spontaneously they say, "Our Lord! We believe.
Inscribe us among the witnesses."

THE TABLE SPREAD 5:83

*A believer is never tired of hearing about good
deeds until he enters Paradise.*

The Prophet Muhammad, as reported by
Abu Sayeed al-Khodri, *Al-Hadis,* 1:121

MARCH 19

Say, "Evil and good are not comparable, even though the abundance of evil may tempt you. Remain observant of Allah, O men of understanding, that you may prosper."

THE TABLE SPREAD 5:100

Be wary of malice, for malice consumes virtues, just as fire consumes fuel.

> The Prophet Muhammad, as reported by
> Abu Hurairah, *Al-Hadis*, 1:499

March 20

Believers! You are accountable only for your own souls. Those who go astray can never harm you if you are on the right path. All shall return to Allah in the end, where He will make known to you all that you earned.

THE TABLE SPREAD 5:105

A wise man works modestly toward the here-after while a foolish man follows his low desires yet expects blessings from Allah.

The Prophet Muhammad, as reported by Shaddad bin Aus, *Al-Hadis,* 1:401

MARCH 21

Then Jesus, the son of Mary, said, "Lord! Send down to us from heaven a table spread with food that it may become a token of a feast for us and for those who will come after us. Let that be a sign of Your benevolence. Provide sustenance for us, O Lord, for You indeed are the best of sustainers."

THE TABLE SPREAD 5:114

"Unless You give no one gives.
O Creator, unlock the gates of your bounty."
He turned his face to heaven and said,
"No one knows my devotion save You.
You put that prayer into my heart.
You raised a hundred hopes."

Rumi, *Mathnawi*, 3:2325, 2331–32

MARCH 22

It was He who created you from clay and decreed a term for you in this world and the next.
Yet still you doubt. He is the only Lord of the
heavens and the earth, completely aware of all
that you conceal and all that you reveal. He
knows what you deserve.

CATTLE 6:2–3

*Live in this world like a stranger, a wayfarer,
and deem yourselves as dwellers of the graves.*

The Prophet Muhammad, as reported by
Ibn Umar, *Al-Hadis,* 1:514

MARCH 23

To Him belongs everything that dwells in the night and in the day. He hears all and is aware of everything. Say, "Why should I then choose any other than Allah as my Protector? He is the Creator of the heavens and the earth, the One who sustains everything but is sustained by none. I was commanded to be the first to submit and not to be of the idolaters."

CATTLE 6:13–14

When you resolve to become pious, the devil in your nature cries out at you: "Tread not those paths, O confused one; distress and poverty will overcome you. You will be despised, let down by friends, you will regret it." Dread of the devil has bound their souls; the cries of the devil are the drover of the damned; the call of the Lord is a guardian of the saints.

Rumi, Mathnawi, 3:4326–28, 4337, 4343

MARCH 24

If Allah afflicts you with hardship, there is none
that can remove it save Him, and if He blesses
you with good fortune, no one can reduce it.
He has power over all things.

CATTLE 6:17

*When you see the misfortune of your brother,
do not rejoice, for Allah may save him and
afflict you with the same misfortune.*

The Prophet Muhammad, as reported by
Wa'silah bin al-Asqa'a, *Al-Hadis,* 1:295

MARCH 25

The life of this world is nothing but a pastime and a sport. Far superior is the life to come for those who are righteous. Then why don't you understand?

CATTLE 6:32

When we are ignorant we live in His prison;
when we become prudent we live in His palace;
when we fall asleep we become intoxicated;
when we are awakened we are in His hands.

Rumi, *Mathnawi*, 1:1510–11

MARCH 26

All the beasts that roam on the earth and all the
birds that soar through the air are but commu-
nities like your own. We have omitted nothing
from the Book. Before their Lord they shall all
be gathered in the end.

CATTLE 6:38

*Do not seek sustenance from people. God is the
real Provider. If He wills a certain person to be
the means of your livelihood, do not consider
that person to be in control of your destiny.
Have faith and be certain in the knowledge that
your daily bread does not depend upon any
mortal, but upon God who created all.*

Al-Hajwiri, *The Kashf al-Mahjub*, p. 106

MARCH 27

Do not dismiss those that call upon their Lord morning and evening, seeking His countenance. You are not accountable for them, just as they are not accountable for you. Then if you drive them away, you yourself may become one of the wrongdoers.

CATTLE 6:52

Those who maintain kinship with the detached, who continue to provide for those who let them down and willingly forgive their oppressors, shall indeed excel both in this world and the next.

The Prophet Muhammad, as reported by
'Uqbah bin Amir, *Al-Hadis*, 1:548

MARCH 28

He holds the keys to all that is hidden from perception; no one but Him has the knowledge thereof. He is aware of all that inhabit the land and dwell in the sea; he knows every leaf that falls. The tiniest grain in the darkest bowels of the earth, everything fresh or arid is recorded in a glorious book of records.

CATTLE 6:59

The Almighty Allah judges you neither by your countenance nor your wealth, but by the purity of your hearts and your deeds.

The Prophet Muhammad, as reported by
Abu Hurairah, *Al-Hadis,* 1:86

MARCH 29

It is He who carries your soul at night and
knows what you accomplish by day. Then at
daytime He rouses you up to life again, that the
span appointed for you may be completed. In
the end you shall all return to Him, and He will
show you the truth of all that you earned.

CATTLE 6:60

*During sleep the spirit is set free. Behold how it
rejoices in the place (of freedom). The wicked is
delivered from his wickedness; the prisoner escapes the sorrow of his confinement. The world
appears wide, but in truth is very narrow. Its
laughter lamentation, its glory shame.*

Rumi, *Mathnawi,* 3:3541–42, 3544

MARCH 30

Say, "Who delivers you from the darkness of the land and the sea? You call upon Him humbly and in silent terror, beseeching Him in secret saying, 'Deliver us from this anguish and we will be truly grateful.'"

CATTLE 6:63

Blessed was the hour that You saw me. I was dead and You gave me a new life. You sought me like a mother; I shunned you like a fool. Happy is he who espies Your face, O You whom pure spirits praise. How I reproached You with many silly words.

Rumi, *Mathnawi*, 2:1897–98, 1991–92

MARCH 31

Those who believe and do not obscure their faith by wrongdoing, shall certainly earn salvation, for they have found the right path.

CATTLE 6:83

When Allah desires the redemption of His people, He causes them to suffer in this world. But when He is averse, He leaves them to transgress until death overtakes.

The Prophet Muhammad, as reported by
Anas bin Malik, *Al-Hadis,* 1:315

APRIL

April 1

It is He who made the stars beacons for you
that you may be guided by them amid the darkness of the land and the sea. We have made
plain Our revelations for people of knowledge.

CATTLE 6:98

*I struggled hard but did not reap the fruits of
my labors. Then I gazed into myself and found
that my ego and my heart were unified. When
the ego and the heart are united, a portion of all
that shines upon the heart is seized by the self.
Thus I came to know the cause of my dilemma,
that the light illuminating my heart was being
seized by my ego.*

Al-Nuri, in *Islamic Sufism,* p. 333

APRIL 2

It is He who sends down water from the sky, with which sprout buds of every kind. From these He brings forth the green vegetation, the thick variegated grain, and the clusters of dates that stem from the palm trees, vineyards, and the groves of olives and pomegranates, which are all so alike yet so different. Behold their fruits when they reach perfection. Indeed in all these are signs for those who believe.

CATTLE 6:100

In separation fertile soil becomes barren,
the pure water stagnant.
Air is sickly, and a pyre turns to ashes.
The orchard once close to Paradise
now festers in disease and decay.
Do not mourn the worldly loss;
ask for your soul to be saved.
Many delighted in what you hold dear.
In the end it left them and became mere wind.
Escape from its love before it escapes you.

Rumi, *Mathnawi*, 3:3690–92,
3696, 3698–99

APRIL 3

The Word of your Lord is perfected in truth and justice. There is none that can change His words. He hears all and knows all.

CATTLE 6:116

The words, "Praise be to Allah," are the easiest to recite, yet heaviest in balance and dearest to the Merciful.

The Prophet Muhammad, as reported by Abu Hurairah, *Al-Hadis*, 3:740

APRIL 4

If you follow the greater majority on earth they would lead you astray. They follow nothing but the conjectures of others and mislead those who follow them. Your Lord knows best who stray from the path of Truth; He knows best who are the rightly guided.

CATTLE 6:117–18

What I fear most for my people are the hypocrites, who talk wisely, yet act unjustly.

The Prophet Muhammad, as reported by
Umar bin al-Khattab, *Al-Hadis,* 1:423

APRIL 5

This is the path of your Lord, a straight path.
We have detailed Our revelations for those who
take heed and have prepared for them an abode
of peace with their Lord. He will be their Protecting Friend as a reward for their good deeds.

CATTLE 6:127–28

*The Prophet once drew a line and said, "This
is the path of faith." Then he drew several lines
on either side and said, "On these lines you
may encounter the devil. But this path of mine
is the straight path. So follow it."*

Reported by Abd'Allah bin Mas'ud,
Al-Hadis, 1:168

APRIL 6

This is a blessed Scripture that We have revealed. So follow it and be righteous, that you may be shown mercy.

CATTLE 6:156

The best among you are those who learn the Qur'an and teach it to others.

The Prophet Muhammad, as reported by Uthman bin Affan, *Al-Hadis,* 3:668

APRIL 7

Say, "Behold, my Lord has guided me onto a straight path, the path of the virtuous Abraham who turned away from all that was false. All my prayers and my devotion, my life and my death are for Allah, the Lord of the worlds, He who has no peer. Thus am I commanded, becoming the first among those that surrender themselves to Him."

CATTLE 6:162–64

Knowledge is light; avarice ice.
Knowledge is water; this world dirt.
A trickle of wisdom appears from beyond
to check the vices of this world.
Should the trickle become abundant,
none would endure, be it virtue or vice.

Rumi, Mathnawi, 1:2068–70

APRIL 8

Then they implored, "Lord! We have wronged our souls. Unless You forgive us and have mercy on us, we shall be among the lost."

THE HEIGHTS 7:23

Sometimes in order to help He makes us cry.
Happy the eye that sheds tears for His sake.
Fortunate the heart that burns for His sake.
Laughter always follows tears.
Blessed are those who understand.
Life blossoms wherever water flows.
Where tears are shed divine mercy is shown.

Rumi, *Mathnawi*, 1:817–20

APRIL 9

Children of Adam! We bestowed raiment upon you to cover your shame, adornments pleasing to the eyes. But the raiment of piety is the finest. Such are among the revelations of Allah, that you may take heed.

THE HEIGHTS 7:26

When you purify your hearts just as you purify your raiment, union with God will follow. You cannot become a Sufi by merely wearing coarse woolen shirts and following strict ritual, pretending to be pious while inside your hearts you bear malice and avarice. A real Sufi has attained a state of perfection on the inside. If you sincerely seek union with God, then seek Him inside your hearts and leave the world alone.

Sheikh Abdul Qadir Jillani,
Fayuz E Yazdani, p. 150

April 10

Say, "My Lord commands you to enjoin impartial justice. Turn to Him wherever you bow down in worship, and call upon Him in complete devotion. Even as He brought you into being, so shall you return to Him."

The Heights 7:29

I realized what was hidden within me
and conversed with You in secret.
Though we were united, we still were apart.
Though awe hid You from my searching eyes,
ecstasy brought You close
to my innermost being.

Al-Hujwiri, The Kashf al-Mahjub, p. 255

April 11

Call on your Lord in humility in the secret of your hearts. He does not love those that transgress; so do not work mischief on the earth after its reformation. Beseech Him both in fear and hope. For Allah's mercy is close to the righteous.

THE HEIGHTS 7:55–56

Your bounty fulfills every need.
Why should we turn to any other?
The scant knowledge that endures in my soul,
deliver it from the wiles of the body's clay
before this clay consumes it away,
before these winds sweep it away.

Rumi, *Mathnawi*, 1:1880, 1883–84

APRIL 12

Moses said to his people, "Seek help from your Lord and remain patient. The earth belongs to the Lord; He gives it as a heritage to those of His servants that He may choose. A promising future awaits the righteous."

THE HEIGHTS 7:128

If you persevere in adversity and depend on God, then know that He will remove your afflictions and bestow vast blessings upon you. For in His Book God promises, "Those who depend upon Allah, Allah bestows His bounty upon them and provides for them from means unknown." Therefore follow the road of patience and rejoice in His infinite bounty.

Sheikh Abdul Qadir Jillani,
Futhul Ghaib, p. 86

APRIL 13

When [Adam and Eve] saw that they had gone astray, they repented and announced, "Unless our Lord have mercy on us and forgive us, we shall indeed be among the lost."

THE HEIGHTS 7:149

His burdens have made him double over, his moans before you are loud and clear. "Show me a prayer, a benediction," he cries, "that I may be delivered from these hidden chains."

Rumi, *Mathnawi*, 3:1668–69

APRIL 14

Then Moses said, "Lord! Have mercy upon me and my brother; grant us Your benevolent mercy, for You are the Most Compassionate of all those who show mercy."

THE HEIGHTS 7:151

He who is given his share of kindness is given his share of good in this world and the here-after.

The Prophet Muhammad, as reported by A'ishah bint Abi Bakr, *Al-Hadis*, 1:339

APRIL 15

Those who transgress but afterward repent and have faith shall certainly find their Lord to be forgiving and merciful.

THE HEIGHTS 7:153

Come, O lover!
Come, let Me ease your suffering.
Let Me be your friend;
let Me improve your state.
Come, O lover!
Come, surrender yourself to Me
that I may give you My life
and make you rejoice once again.

Rumi, *The Life and Thought of Rumi*, p. 129

APRIL 16

Allah's are the most beautiful names. Invoke Him by them, and leave the company of those who blaspheme His names. They shall soon be requited for what they do.

THE HEIGHTS 7:180

There are ninety-nine names that are attributed to Allah. Those who invoke them shall enter Paradise.

The Prophet Muhammad, as reported by Abu Hurairah, *Al-Hadis,* 3:736

APRIL 17

Show forgiveness, enjoin kindness, and stay
away from the ignorant. If Satan ever tempts
you, then seek refuge in Allah. He hears all
and knows all. When temptation troubles those
who guard against evil, they have but to remember Allah and they shall behold light.

THE HEIGHTS 7:199–201

Seek a true friend,
for a friend seeks the benefit of a friend,
Do good to the people for the sake of God
or for the peace of your own soul
that you may always see what is pure
and save your heart from the darkness of hate.

Rumi, *Mathnawi*, 4:1972, 1979–80

APRIL 18

When the Qur'an is recited, listen to it and pay heed, that you may obtain mercy and remember your Lord within your hearts with humility and awe below your breath, in the morning and in the evening; and do not be heedless.

THE HEIGHTS 7:204–5

The Merciful God promised Mustafa,[9]
"You will die but the Qur'an will prevail.
I shall exalt your Book and its Miracle
and protect its face from being changed.
This Qur'an to you is Moses' staff;
like that dragon it will devour all deception."

Rumi, *Mathnawi*, 3:1197–98, 1209

APRIL 19

Those who are close to the Lord do not scorn
His service. They praise Him and glorify Him
and prostrate themselves before Him.

THE HEIGHTS 7:206

*During prostration a servant draws nearest to
the Lord, so augment your devotions.*

The Prophet Muhammad, as reported by
Abu Hurairah, *Al-Hadis,* 3:286

April 20

True believers are those whose hearts are roused with awe when Allah is mentioned, whose faith grows and is fortified when they hear His revelations recited before them. They place all their trust in their Lord.

THE SPOILS OF WAR 8:2

Those who truly know God worship Him with all their resolve; they concede to His ubiquitous bounty and obey all His commandments with the utmost fervor. As their adoration grows so does their obedience, since they are aware that this world is a madhouse and its inhabitants madmen wearing shackles of lust and chains of sin.

Al-Hujwiri, *The Kashf al-Mahjub*, p. 98

APRIL 21

True believers are those who establish worship and donate in alms of what We have bestowed upon them. They will be exonerated and exalted by their Lord, and a bountiful provision will be conferred upon them.

SPOILS OF WAR 8:3–4

When people gather and remember Allah, the angels surround them and blessings encompass them. Peace descends on them and Allah mentions them to those near Him.[10]

The Prophet Muhammad, as reported by Abu Hurairah, *Al-Hadis*, 3:722

APRIL 22

When you implored the help of your Lord, He responded, "I shall send for your assistance a thousand angels, rank upon rank." This was a message of hope from your Lord to reassure and comfort your hearts, since victory comes only through the help of Allah, the Mighty, the Wise.

THE SPOILS OF WAR 8:9–10

Do not lose hope in Allah, for He is the Creator. He will create another way for you. Do not flee from your trials; patience in adversity is the foundation of all virtue, of compassion and sainthood. Patience is the foundation, and without a sound foundation you cannot build a monument.

Sheikh Abdul Qadir Jillani,
Fayuz E Yazdani, p. 83

APRIL 23

Remember when you were few and considered feeble in the land and lived in constant fear of persecution. He gave you refuge and strengthened you with His help and provided you with good things that you might be grateful. Believers, do not betray Allah and His messenger, and do not knowingly betray your trust. Remember that your possessions and your children are but a test, and Allah's reward is immense.

THE SPOILS OF WAR 8:26–28

The bottom of the river is full of jewels.
Take heed! Do not make the water turbid.
The spirit of man is like the air:
when dust surrounds it the sky is veiled.
Notwithstanding such a state of darkness,
God made visions to help you
find the road to redemption.

Rumi, *Mathnawi*, 4:2483–84, 2486

April 24

Believers, if you abide by your obligations to Allah, He will furnish you with wisdom and will absolve you of your evil thoughts and deeds and will relent toward you. Allah is of infinite bounty.

THE SPOILS OF WAR 8:29

How numerous Your favors bestowed upon me, favors of gifts and grace and assistance. Your love is now my only desire and my ultimate bliss.

Rabi'a, in *Rabi'a the Mystic*, p. 28

APRIL 25

Obey the commandments of Allah and His messenger, and do not dispute with one another lest you falter and your strength depart from you; be steadfast, for Allah helps the steadfast.

THE SPOILS OF WAR 8:46

Had the world been conceived just to praise God, there would be no fervor in glorifying God. Equip man with a sword, remove his infirmities, and see what he will be: a brave knight or a devious thief?

Rumi, The Life and Thought of Rumi, p. 160

April 26

Those who remained devout and left their homes and strove with their wealth and lives for Allah's sake shall be held in high regard by their Lord. These indeed shall prosper; give them good tidings of His mercy and of a paradise where an everlasting bliss shall be theirs.

REPENTANCE 9:20–21

Once a rich merchant, seeing Rabi'a's house falling into disrepair, gave her a thousand pieces of gold and a new house.... Immediately she returned the money to the merchant and said, "I fear I will become attached to this house and will no longer be able to occupy myself with the other world. My only desire is to be of service to God."

Rabi'a, in *Rabi'a the Mystic,* p. 86.

APRIL 27

Say, "Nothing shall afflict us except what Allah has ordained for us. He is our Protecting Friend. In Allah let the believers place all their trust."

REPENTANCE 9:51

Have faith in God the Omnipotent,
the Eternal, the First and the Last,
who grants life and determines death.
He bestows bounty,
and only He can restore crushed hopes.
Have faith, do not lose hope, wait patiently.
He indeed will create a way
to deliver you from your hardships.

Sheikh Abdul Qadir Jillani,
Fayuz E Yazdani, p. 74

APRIL 28

Then there are those who confess to their sins. They had combined good deeds with evil ones. Yet it is possible that Allah may accept their repentance and relent toward them, for Allah is forgiving and merciful. Accept their alms that they may be cleansed and purified, and pray for them; for your prayer will bring them immense comfort. Allah hears all and knows all.

REPENTANCE 9:102–3

Behold the containers before the pharmacist. Kind assorted beside kind. The containers shattered; all the souls scattered. Good and evil intermingled. Then God sent Apostles with His revelations to arrange the grains inside the containers.

Rumi, *Mathnawi*, 2:280, 283–84

April 29

Those that turn to Him in repentance, those who praise Him and those who serve Him, those who fast and those who bow down and prostrate before Him, those who enjoin uprightness and forbid evil, and those who conform to the commandments of Allah shall certainly triumph. Give the glad tidings to all the believers!

REPENTANCE 9:112

When the ocean of Mercy begins to foam,
even stones drink the water of life.
The face of earth becomes lush green,
the dead wood springs to life,
the lamb and the wolf together play,
the despairing becomes valiant and strong.

Rumi, *Mathnawi,* 5:2882, 2885–86

APRIL 30

It is He who gave the sun his splendor and the moon her light, determining her phases that you may learn to compute the years and to measure time. Allah created these only to make the truth manifest. He makes these revelations explicit for those who have knowledge.

JONAH 10:5

The servile earth and the lofty sky:
without this opposite
the sky would not be so high.
The low and high of the earth
are winter and spring.
The low and high of time
are night and day.
The low and high of the body
are sickness and health.
By means of these opposites
the world is kept alive;
by means of these doubles
souls feel fear and hope.

Rumi, *Mathnawi*, 6:1848–51, 1853

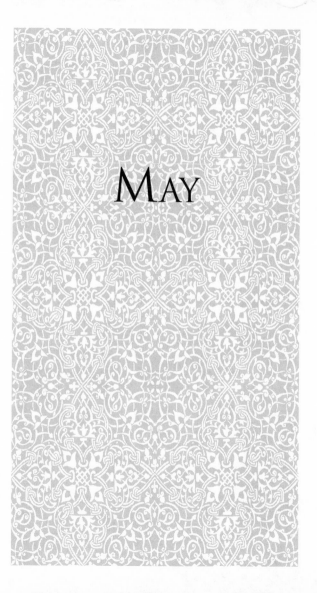

MAY

MAY 1

Allah invites you to the abode of peace and guides whom He will to a straight path.

JONAH 10:25

The Lord Almighty ordained, "Find leisure for My service and I shall fill your hearts with peace and enrich you in bounty."

The Prophet Muhammad, as reported by
Abu Hurairah, *Al-Hadis*, 1:450

MAY 2

If they renounce you, say, "My deeds are mine, and your deeds are yours. You are not accountable for what I do, and I am not accountable for what you do."

JONAH 10:41

Both Moses and Pharaoh
dwell within your being.
Seek these opponents within your being.
The conception of Moses is a reawakening.
The light is the same,
though the lamp is different.

Rumi, *The Life and Thought*
of Rumi, p. 163

MAY 3

Humankind, an admonition has been sent from your Lord. It is a balm for all that ails the heart, a source of guidance to grace the true believers. So let them rejoice in the bounty of Allah. It transcends what they hoard.

JONAH 10:57–58

There is a key for everything, and the key to Paradise is love for the poor.

The Prophet Muhammad, as reported by
Ibn Umar, *Al-Hadis,* 1:280

May 4

Verily those devoted to Allah shall have no fear, nor shall they grieve. Those who believe and strive in the way of Allah shall rejoice both in this world and in the life of the hereafter. Nothing shall alter the Word of Allah; that is the Supreme Triumph.

JONAH 10:62–64

I saw a man in Paradise for a deed as simple as cutting down a tree that stood in the middle of a road, causing wayfarers much distress.

The Prophet Muhammad, as reported by Ibn Umar, *Al-Hadis*, 1:325

MAY 5

Do not let their speech grieve you. For all glory is Allah's. He hears all and knows all.

JONAH 10:65

The rank of a man of silence is better than divine service for sixty years.

The Prophet Muhammad, as reported by 'Imran bin Hussain, *Al-Hadis,* 1:460

MAY 6

They said, "In Allah we place our trust. Lord! Do not let us suffer at the hands of the transgressors. Deliver us through Your grace, our Lord, from those who deny the Truth."

JONAH 10:85–86

Do not regard yourself as infamous or weak.
Reflect upon your aspirations, O noble one.
No matter what your station be,
keep searching.
For this pursuit is a blessed course.
This quest removes all impediments to God.

Rumi, *The Life and Thought*
of Rumi, p. 166

MAY 7

Allah replied, "Your prayer has been heard.
Follow the straight path, and do not follow the
path of the ignorant."

JONAH 10:89

*When your heart becomes a seat of secrets, you
will come to your destination. Hide your innermost thoughts, said the Prophet, and you will
attain your object of desire. Seeds are buried in
the earth, but their inmost secrets bloom as an
exquisite garden.*

Rumi, *Mathnawi,* 1:175–77

MAY 8

Say, "Humankind! The Truth has come to you from your Lord. He that follows the right path follows it for the good of his own soul, and whosoever goes astray does so to his own detriment. I am not a warder over you."

JONAH 10:108

Doubt is a precipice on the way to God. Blessed is he who is freed from its bonds. He who fares without any doubt, adhere to his footprints if you do not know the way. Cleave to the footprints of the deer and advance with care that you may reach the musk-gland. By means of such trekking, even if you walk on fire, you will reach the luminous peak.

Rumi, Mathnawi, 3:490–93

May 9

Abide by what has been revealed to you and forbear until Allah makes known His judgment, for He is the best of Judges.

JONAH 10:109

He complained of his pain a hundredfold. God said, "Grief and pain make you modest and noble. Your real enemy is your own medicine, the elixir that seeks to win your heart. Flee from it to solitude and seek the help of God's grace. Your friends are really your enemies, for they occupy you and make you oblivious of God."

Rumi, *Mathnawi,* 4:91–92, 94–96

MAY 10

There is not a beast on the earth whose sustenance does not depend on Allah. He knows its
habitation and its repository. All is in a clear
record.

HUD 11:6

*Since I understood four things, I have discarded
all other knowledge. First, that my daily sustenance has already been apportioned to me and
will neither increase nor decrease by my futile
efforts, so I strive to increase it no more. Second, I alone and no one else can atone for my
sins, so I devote myself to the Lord. Third, I
know that I will never be able to escape death,
which is in our pursuit, so I have prepared myself to meet him. Fourth, I know that God is
observing me; therefore I refrain from doing
what I must not do.*

Hatim al-Asamm,
The Kashf al-Mahjub, p. 13

May 11

And when We bestow grace upon them after their misfortunes they say, "All our sorrows have departed." And they become exultant and boastful. But the steadfast who persevere in adversity and work good deeds shall find forgiveness and a noteworthy reward waiting for them.

HUD 11:10–11

Prostrating himself he cried, "You indeed are the noble one; I, the ignoble, feel abashed on your account. You are perfect and still remain obedient to His command; and I, barely a fraction, remain unjust, wicked, and unguided. You are perfect, yet are humble and fear the Lord; and I, the tainted, am averse and hostile."

Rumi, *Mathnawi*, 5:128-30

May 12

Those who believe and remain righteous and humble themselves before their Lord are the rightful owners of the Garden; therein will they abide.

Hud 11:23

The wisdom of this world brings doubt. The wisdom of religion soars above the skies. Reflection on Truth opens the way to the kingdom. Treasures and armies do not make a king. A true king is a king within himself.

Rumi, *Mathnawi*, 2:3203; 3207–8

MAY 13

Noah said, "My Lord! I seek refuge in You from asking You about things I have no knowledge of. Unless You forgive me and have mercy on me I shall indeed be among the lost."

HUD 11:47

I seek refuge in Allah from knowledge that brings no wisdom, from a heart that lacks kindness, from desires that bring discontent, and from supplications that go unanswered.

The Prophet Muhammad, as reported by Abu Hurairah, *Al-Hadis,* 3:790

MAY 14

My people! Seek forgiveness of your Lord, and turn to Him repentant. He will cause the sky to rain abundance on you and will add to your strength. Do not go back to transgression!

HUD 11:52

A man went back to transgressing after he had sincerely asked forgiveness of God and swore never to sin again. "How will God forgive me this time?" he asked in despair.

A heavenly voice responded, "You obeyed Me and I made amends for you, then you abandoned Me and I indulged you, and now that you returned to Me I shall receive you."

Al-Hujwiri, *The Kashf al-Mahjub*, p. 298

May 15

I have placed my trust in Allah, who is my Lord and also yours. There is not a living creature whose destiny He does not control. Verily! My Lord's is the Straight Path.

HUD 11:56

Blessed are the ones who rely on Allah and have surrendered themselves before His will, who are grateful in prosperity and patient in adversity.

The Prophet Muhammad, as reported by
Shu'aib bin Se'nam, *Al-Hadis*, 1:123

MAY 16

They said, "Do you wonder at the command-
ment of Allah? His mercy and His blessings be
upon you, O people of the house! Indeed He is
worthy of all praise and glory!"

HUD 11:73

*God scatters His light over all spirits. The for-
tunate hold up their skirts to receive it. Those
who receive His light turn from all except God.
Without the skirt of love, we cannot receive
our share.*

Rumi, *Mathnawi*, 1:760–62

MAY 17

My people! Weigh goods justly and give full measure; do not defraud people of their property, nor befoul the land by spreading evil.

HUD 11:85

Practice what you have learned, for theory without practice is like a spirit without a body. One who is content with learning alone is not learned, for the truly learned seek more than mere words. Divine guidance entails self-mortification, without which contemplation is unattainable.

Al-Hujwiri, *The Kashf al-Mahjub*, p. 95

May 18

Turn to the Lord in repentance and implore Him to forgive you. My Lord is indeed the Most Compassionate, the Most Merciful.

HUD 11:90

Allah accepts repentance, as long as it is not at the time of death.

The Prophet Muhammad, as reported by
Ibn Umar, *Al-Hadis,* 3:760

MAY 19

Establish worship at the two ends of the day and in some watches of the night. Good deeds annul ill deeds. This is a reminder for those who pay heed.

HUD 11:114

Every night during a certain hour the blessings of both this world and the next are bestowed upon those who seek.

The Prophet Muhammad, as reported by Ja'bir bin Abd'Allah, *Al-Hadis,* 3:402

MAY 20

Have patience; Allah does not deny the reward of the righteous.

HUD 11:115

Give your life for that cup of divine wisdom. How can you succeed without endurance and patience? To wait for the sake of that cup is no hardship. Show patience, for patience is the key to joy.

Rumi, *Mathnawi*, 3:211–12

MAY 21

Allah alone has the knowledge of the mysteries of the heavens and the earth; all matter will return to Him. So worship Him and place your trust in Him. Your Lord is aware of what you do.

HUD 11:123

Upon death everyone will be questioned by the angels in regard to their deeds on the earth, while their successors will be preoccupied with their mundane belongings.

The Prophet Muhammad, as reported by
Abu Hurairah, *Al-Hadis,* 2:736

MAY 22

You shall be the chosen of your Lord; He will enlighten you to comprehend and interpret visions and will bestow His grace upon you and upon the house of Jacob, as He perfected His blessings upon your forefathers, Abraham and Isaac. Your Lord indeed is the Discerning, All-Aware.

JOSEPH 12:6

If your dream brings you joy, take it as a blessing from your Lord. Express gratitude and share it with others. However, if it incites fear, then remember it is but an assault from Satan. Seek refuge in Allah from its evil and do not mention it to anyone, for that shall annul any harm intended to you.

The Prophet Muhammad, as reported by Abu Sayeed al-Khodri, *Sahih al-Bukhari,* p. 1014

MAY 23

Joseph turned to his Lord and said, "My Lord, I would rather go to prison than give in to their lure. Unless You protect me from their wiles, I may yield to their charms and fall from grace." So the Lord heard his prayer and fended off their wiles from him. Indeed He is All-Knowing, All-Aware.

JOSEPH 12:33-34

Lord! I depend upon You alone;
in You I place my faith.
I seek refuge in You,
for there is no God but You.
Only You, my Lord, are the Infinite;
all else shall pass away.

The Prophet Muhammad, as reported by
Abd'Allah ibn Abbas, *Al-Hadis,* 3:790

MAY 24

He said, "I complain of my grief and anguish only to Allah. The Lord has made known to me things that you have no knowledge of. My sons, go in search of Joseph and his brother, and do not despair of Allah's mercy. Only those who do not believe lose hope in His loving kindness."

JOSEPH 12:86–87

The spiritual path ruins the body, but subsequently restores it to health. It ruins the house to reveal the treasure, and with that treasure it builds better than before.

Rumi, *Mathnawi*, 1:306–7

MAY 25

My Lord! You endowed me with power and taught me to interpret dreams. Creator of the heavens and the earth! You are my only Protecting Friend in this world and the hereafter. Allow me to die in submission and admit me among the righteous.

JOSEPH 12:101

At midnight I say, "I am near you: be not afraid of the night, for I am your protecting friend." Last night in your dream you saw One with a prayer-rug. That was I, and what I told you in that dream about the meaning of prophecy: make those words of Mine your mind's guide.

Rumi, *Mathnawi*, 2:3574, 3586–88

MAY 26

It was Allah who raised the heavens without visible supports, and then established His glory on the Throne. He compelled the sun and the moon to be of service, each running an appointed term; He ordains the course of all things. He made these revelations manifest, that you may be certain of meeting your Lord.

THE THUNDER 13:2

God made the illusion look real and the real an illusion. He concealed the sea and made the foam visible, the wind invisible, and the dust manifest. You see the dust whirling, but how can the dust rise by itself? You see the foam, but not the ocean. Invoke Him with deeds, not words, for deeds are real and will save you in the afterlife.

Rumi, *Mathnawi*, 5:1026–28, 1030, 1044, 1050

MAY 27

It is He who spread the earth wide and placed therein mountains and rivers. He created all the plants and distinguished them with their male and female parts. He conceals the night with the day. Behold, in all these there are portents for those who pay heed.

THE THUNDER 13:3

I implored the sage in earnest last night
to unveil the mysteries of the universe.
He whispered softly in my ear,
"Silence!
It is something to perceive but never to say."

Rumi, The Life and Thought
of Rumi, p. 129

MAY 28

It is He who raises the heavy clouds and causes the lightning to flash, inspiring you with fear and hope. The thunder hymns His praise, as do the angels in awe of Him. He alone hurls the thunderbolt at whom He will, yet they stubbornly argue about Allah. Allah is the Almighty.

THE THUNDER 13:12–13

Fear and hope are two pillars of faith. By practicing either one of them a person will not fall into error, because both fear and hope lead to union. Those who fear devote themselves to God through fear of separation from Him, and those who hope worship in hope of realizing the ultimate union.

Al-Razi, *The Kashf al-Mahjub,* p. 122

MAY 29

Peace be with you, for you persevered steadfastly. How blessed is the final abode!

THE THUNDER 13:24

God kindles the fire of love in the hearts of
the chosen, so that their carnal selves are consumed. Once ignited the fire of longing never
dies. That is the flame about which the Prophet
said, "When God wills the good of his servant,
He kindles a light of faith in his heart."

When they asked him what were the signs of
that fire, he replied, "Deviation from the abode
of vanity; progression toward the Eternal."

Abu Sa'id, in *Rabi'a the Mystic*, p. 90

MAY 30

Those who believe and have faith, their hearts are comforted by the remembrance of Allah. Verily in the remembrance of Allah shall all hearts find peace.

THE THUNDER 13:28

The Almighty Allah says,
"When a servant thinks of Me, I am near.
When he invokes Me, I am with him.
If he reflects on Me in secret, I reply in secret,
and if he acknowledges Me in an assembly,
I acknowledge him in a far superior assembly."

The Prophet Muhammad, as reported by
Abu Hurairah, *Al-Hadis,* 3:723

MAY 31

Those who believe and work good deeds shall be blessed with joy; bliss shall be their journey's end.

THE THUNDER 13:29

Those admitted to Paradise shall experience true bliss. Never shall they know want, nor will they suffer old age.

The Prophet Muhammad, as reported by Abu Hurairah, *Al-Hadis*, 4:165

JUNE

JUNE 1

Behold how Allah sets forth the parable of a good word being like a good tree, its roots set firm, its branches reaching into heaven, its fruit prolific in every season by permission of its Lord. Allah sets these parables before humankind that they may reflect.

ABRAHAM 14:24–25

Every good deed is charity whether you come to your brother's assistance or just greet him with a smile.

The Prophet Muhammad, as reported by
Ja'bir bin Abd'Allah, *Al-Hadis,* 1:300

JUNE 2

He grants you everything that you ask of Him. If you were to count the blessings conferred upon you by the Lord, you could never reckon them. Yet humankind persists in wrongdoing, remaining forever ungrateful.

ABRAHAM 14:34

When Moses conversed with God, he asked, "Lord, where shall I seek You?"

God answered, "Among the brokenhearted."

Moses continued, "But, Lord, no heart could be more despairing than mine."

And God replied, "Then I am where you are."

Abu'l-Fayd al-Misri,
The Kashf al-Mahjub, p. 101

JUNE 3

Lord! Allow me and my descendants to remain steadfast in devotion. Lord! Humbly I implore that You accept my pleas.

ABRAHAM 14:40

The lower soul dissuades from conforming to faith. The more the self is subdued, the easier it becomes to glorify God. When the ego is annihilated, worship becomes sustenance, just as it sustains the angels.

Al-Hujwiri, *The Kashf al-Mahjub*, p. 303

JUNE 4

Lord! Forgive me and my parents and all the devoted on the Day of Reckoning.

ABRAHAM 14:41

Once Abu Umamah asked the Prophet about the rights of parents over their children. The Prophet replied, "They are your Paradise and they are your Hell."

Reported by Abu Umamah,
Al-Hadis, 1:187

JUNE 5

Every blessing is held in store with Us, and We alone send it down in determined measures.

AL-HIJR 15:21

In the treasure house of blessings there is also a store of afflictions. But most lack patience and begin to lament their misfortune before all and sundry, hoping to receive succor. Do they not know that none has the power to help or harm, be they friends or enemies? In their lack of faith such persons deem mortals equal to God. Do they forget that faith in the transient will only hamper their deliverance?

Sheikh Abdul Qadir Jillani,
Fayuz E Yazdani, p. 152

JUNE 6

By His ordinance He sends down the angels
with the Spirit of His divine inspiration to those
among His servants that He chooses, enjoining them: "Warn humankind that there is no
other God save Me. Therefore remain devoted
to Me."

THE BEE 16:2

*The Prophet said, "When you pass by the
Gardens of Paradise rejoice."*

*When his companions asked the location of
those gardens, he replied, "They are the circles
of dhikr."*[11]

The Prophet Muhammad, as reported by
Anas bin Malik, *Al-Hadis*, 3:729

JUNE 7

Allah alone guides to the straight path, for many paths swerve away from it. Had Allah willed, He would have guided all of you.

THE BEE 16:9

In the hour of grief you turn to Him;
when grief departs you transgress.
In adversity you moan entreating Him;
when ease returns you turn away.
Those who know God remain steady,
but those who doubt exult at times
and become despondent at others.

Rumi, *Mathnawi*, 3:1141–44

JUNE 8

It is He who sends down water from the sky, supplying you with your drink and from it the verdant pastures upon which your cattle feed. And by His leave the crops, olives, dates, grapes, and all kinds of fruits flourish. Indeed in all these there are signs for those who reflect.

THE BEE 16:10–11

Once Rabi'a saw a man with a compress tied around his head. She asked what ailed him.

"My head hurts," he replied.

"How old are you?" she inquired.

"Thirty." Then she asked him if he had suffered a greater part of his life.

"No," he replied.

"For thirty years God endowed you with good health," she said, "but you never displayed a bandage of gratitude, and for one night of pain you bind your head with this compress of complaint."

Rabi'a, in *Rabi'a the Mystic,* p. 61

June 9

It is He who constrained the sea to be of service to you that you may eat fresh fish from it and brings forth from its depths ornaments that you wear. Behold the ships plowing through the waves so that you may seek of His bounty. Be grateful therefore for all His blessings.

The Bee 16:14

With the divine solace "Be not afraid" all fear of oceans or waves or foam should be gone. Rejoice in Him and nothing else. He is the spring; everything else is desolate ice.

Rumi, Mathnawi, 3:494, 507

JUNE 10

Should you ever try to count the blessings of Allah, you would never be able to reckon them. Indeed Allah is the Most Forgiving, the Most Compassionate.

THE BEE 16:18

Those who believe everything to be created by God see Him in everything. They find comfort in regarding the Creator and not His creation. All problems stem from the illusion that created things hold the ultimate power. Turn to Him, therefore, if you seek deliverance.

Al-Nuri, *The Kashf al-Mahjub*, p. 132

JUNE 11

When the righteous are asked, "What has your Lord revealed?" they reply, "That which is indeed the greatest." Those who endure will be blessed with a good fortune in this world, but far superior shall be the abode of the hereafter. Blessed indeed shall be the abode of the righteous.

THE BEE 16:30

Believers are like mirrors for each other.
Like brothers they ward off evil together
and protect each other's backs.

The Prophet Muhammad, as reported by
Abu Hurairah, *Al-Hadis*, 1:297–98

JUNE 12

When We intend a thing, We only need to say the word, "Be," and it is.

THE BEE 16:40

Seek self-discipline with all your soul. Devote yourself to worship and save your soul. Be grateful that God gave you the gift of self-discipline, for you had no power over it. He inspired it within you with the command "Be!"

Rumi, Mathnawi, 3:3395, 3397

JUNE 13

Those who are forced to flee their homes suffering oppression in the cause of Allah shall certainly be compensated with considerable lodgings in the world, but the reward of the hereafter will be far greater, if they but knew.

THE BEE 16:41

Rejoice in sorrow; it will unite you with God.
Bow down and reach the highest peak.
Turn inward, toward the heart,
and delight in the green shade of trees
and many gushing springs.

Rumi, *Mathnawi*, 3:509, 516

JUNE 14

Have they not observed all things created by Allah, how their shadows incline to the right and to the left, prostrating themselves before Allah in humility? All creatures in the heavens and on the earth and also the angels prostrate themselves before Allah; they are not contemptuous.

THE BEE 16:48

Angles were created without lust and evil, the worst obstacles of humankind. Those who despite their evil nature remain pious excel angels in rank. Enthused by their purity angels denounced the human race, so God chose three angels to go to the earth and reform its inhabitants. One angel, espying the corruption, begged God to let him return. The other two, in their earthly form, gave in to lust and fell from grace. Thus God revealed to the other angels the superiority of the devout.

Al-Hujwiri, *The Kashf al-Mahjub*, pp. 240–41

JUNE 15

Allah has conferred all your blessings upon you, and when misfortune befalls you, it is He whom you implore for help.

THE BEE 16:53

The object of search is never withheld from the seeker. Thus the sun is paired with heat and the cloud with water. This present world is the Creator's prison. You chose to invite punishment, so suffer punishment! God said, "To whom We bestowed a particular disposition, We also sent the appropriate provision."

Rumi, *Mathnawi*, 6:1889–90, 1903

JUNE 16

Have they not seen the birds constrained in mid-air? None sustains them save Allah. Verily in this there are signs for those who believe.

THE BEE 16:79

If you rely upon Allah, trusting Him completely, He certainly would provide for you as He provides for the birds. The birds set out hungry in the morning, yet return satisfied at dusk.

The Prophet Muhammad, as reported by Umar bin al-Khattab, *Al-Hadis,* 1:445

JUNE 17

By means of what He created Allah gave you
shelter from the sun and carved out caverns in
the mountains for your refuge. He gave you the
ability to make garments that protect you from
heat, as well as coats of mail that protect you
in warfare. Thus He perfected His favors to
you that you may surrender yourselves before
His will.

THE BEE 16:81

*The only possessions of Jesus were a cup and a
comb. The cup he threw away when he saw a
man drinking water in the palms of his hands,
and the comb when he saw a man use his fin-
gers to smooth out his hair. The coarse woolen
garment of Moses and the poverty of Muhammad are perfect examples for those who seek
guidance.*

Al-Hujwiri, *The Kashf al-Mahjub*, p. 40

JUNE 18

Allah enjoins justice and kindness, and in giving alms to kinsfolk, He forbids indecency and abomination and oppression. He exhorts you that you may take heed.

THE BEE 16:90

Beware! Do not let avarice waylay you!
Do not let greed tear you up by the roots!
For as you sleep,
the stench of your spurious deeds
is thundering on the azure sky.

Rumi, *Mathnawi*, 3:142, 164

JUNE 19

Whoever does right, whether male or female, and is a believer shall most certainly be rewarded for the noblest of their deeds and shall be blessed with a good life.

THE BEE 16:97

Once a harlot came upon a dog dying of thirst. Without a second thought she took off her leather sock,[12] tied it to her veil, got water from a well nearby, and saved the animal's life. For that one act of kindness she was absolved of all her ill deeds. Indeed every deed of kindness toward living beings shall be rewarded.

The Prophet Muhammad, as reported by Abu Hurairah, *Al-Hadis,* 1:329

JUNE 20

When reciting the Qur'an, seek refuge from Satan the outcast. He has no power over those who believe and place their trust in their Lord.

THE BEE 16:98–99

Read the Qur'an as long as you are attentive, but when you feel your attention slip, put the Book away.

The Prophet Muhammad, as reported by Jundub bin Abd'Allah, *Al-Hadis,* 3:696

JUNE 21

Say: "The Holy Spirit revealed the Qur'an from your Lord in truth to strengthen the faith of the believers, to guide them, and to give good tidings to those who have surrendered themselves before to Allah."

THE BEE 16:102

All Muslims, pious or not, are bidden to listen to the recitation of the Qur'an. As God says, "When the Qur'an is recited, listen to it and be silent so that you might attain mercy."

Al-Hujwiri, *The Kashf al-Mahjub*, p. 396

JUNE 22

Nourish yourselves with the good and the lawful victuals that Allah has provided for you, and be grateful of the bounty of your Lord if it is Him you truly serve.

THE BEE 16:114

I am the Word of God living through His Essence. I am the Food of the soul, the Spirit of purity. I am the Fountain of the Water of Life. I deliver the lovers of God from death. If your greed had not raised such a stench, God would have poured a remedy of water on your graves. I accept the warning of the Sage; I will not allow my heart to be sickened by ridicule.

Rumi, *Mathnawi*, 3:4287–91

JUNE 23

Those who commit evil in ignorance but afterward repent and mend their ways shall find the Lord forgiving and merciful.

THE BEE 16:119

Those who steadily seek absolution shall find that the Lord eases their way out of every difficulty, providing for them from unimaginable bounty.

The Prophet Muhammad, as reported by Abd'Allah ibn Abbas, *Al-Hadis*, 3:759

JUNE 24

Indeed this Qur'an guides you to that which is most upright and gives good tidings to the believers who do good works, that theirs shall be a great reward.

THE CHILDREN OF ISRAEL 17:9

The words of the Qur'an have both an outer and an inner meaning, the latter overpowering. Do not regard the surface alone, for the devil never regarded Adam as mere clay. The surface meaning of the Qur'an is like a human torso, features visible, but the spirit hidden.

Rumi, *Mathnawi*, 3:2244, 2247–48

JUNE 25

Every person's deeds have been fastened to his own neck, and on the Day of Resurrection We shall bring them before him in the form of a book which he will find wide open. And he will be told, "Read your book. Your own soul is sufficient this day to call you to account."

THE CHILDREN OF ISRAEL 17:13–14

On the Day of Resurrection, people will be judged according to their intentions.

The Prophet Muhammad, as reported by Abu Hurairah, *Al-Hadis,* 1:87

JUNE 26

Whoever does right, it is for the good of his own soul, but he who goes astray errs only to his own disadvantage. No soul shall bear another's burden. We never punish until We have sent our messenger to forewarn.

THE CHILDREN OF ISRAEL 17:15

Whenever you are tempted by this world, picture a derelict covered with filth whose noxious odor is intolerable. Reviled you will shut your senses to the offensive sight. In the like manner stay away from abomination of sin that may deface your purity. The Lord shall bless you with much bounty; therefore let not the cares of this world drive your peace away.

Sheikh Abdul Qadir Jillani,
Futhul Ghaib, p. 20

JUNE 27

Your Lord is best aware of what is in your hearts. If you are righteous, then you shall find Him most munificent toward those who turn to Him.

THE CHILDREN OF ISRAEL 17:25

Those who intend to do a good deed but cannot follow through shall be rewarded for their intentions.

The Prophet Muhammad, as reported by Anas bin Malik, *Al-Hadis,* 1:87,

JUNE 28

Do not strut on the earth filled with pride, for you cannot rend the earth asunder, nor can you reach the mountains in height.

THE CHILDREN OF ISRAEL 17:37

Little by little God takes beauty away. Little by little life's luster decays. Listen to the passage, "To whom We grant a long life, those We cause to decline." Seek the essence and not the structure. The beauty of heart shall forever abide, for it is enriched with the water of life.

Rumi, *Mathnawi*, 2:714–16

JUNE 29

The seven heavens and the earth and all the creatures that dwell therein glorify Him. There is not a thing that does not celebrate His praise; yet you do not understand their praise. Indeed, He is the Clement, the Merciful.

THE CHILDREN OF ISRAEL 17:44

Worship is like a work of art mastered only by the sincere, the learned scholars who practice what they know, who live and walk among people like everyone else, but in their hearts they seek freedom in the serenity of the wilderness. Because of this yearning they continue to grow until their spirits soar and become united with the numinous. About such God says, "Indeed they are the finest of human beings, cherished by Us."

Sheikh Abdul Qadir Jillani,
Fayuz E Yazdani, p. 399

JUNE 30

On the day He will summon you before Him, you will all respond by praising Him, thinking all the while that you stayed on the earth but a short while. So tell His servants to speak with courtesy and gentleness. For Satan sows discord among them, and Satan is but man's open foe.

THE CHILDREN OF ISRAEL 17:52–53

Every prophet to the world came alone,
within him carrying a hundred unseen worlds.
The cosmos was charmed by his depth
and folded itself into his modest frame.
The foolish thought he was lonely and weak.
With the King as his companion,
how is he weak?

Rumi, *Mathnawi*, 1:2505–7

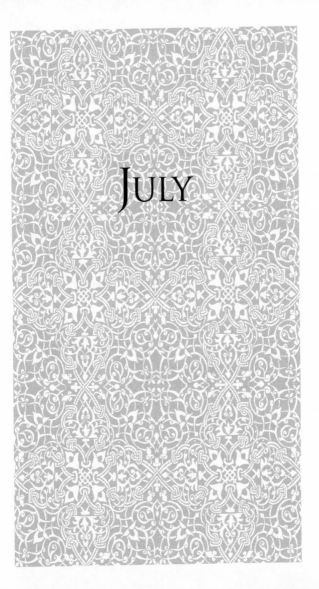

JULY

JULY 1

We have honored the children of Adam. We guided them on land and sea and made provisions for them and exalted them above many of Our creatures.

THE CHILDREN OF ISRAEL 17:70

We honored man by the gift of free will.
Half of him is honeybee, the other half snake.
True believers are stores of honey.
Stores of poison are those who do not believe.

Rumi, *Mathnawi*, 3:3291–92

July 2

Establish worship at sunset until the darkness of the night and recite the Qur'an at dawn, for the recitation of the Qur'an at dawn is witnessed by all that is holy.

THE CHILDREN OF ISRAEL 17:78

The recitation of the Qur'an is witnessed by the angels of the night and the angels of the day.

The Prophet Muhammad, as reported by Abu Hurairah, *Al-Hadis,* 3:167

JULY 3

Say, "Truth has come and falsehood has vanished. For falsehood was bound to vanish." We
revealed the Qur'an that it might heal souls and
bestow grace upon those who believe, though it
adds to the loss of the wrongdoers.

THE CHILDREN OF ISRAEL 17:81–82

*The Lord illumined the hearts of the pious with
the light of certainty that gave them the vision to comprehend the light of all the faiths
of the world.*

Abu'l-Hasan, *The Kashf al-Mahjub*, p. 145

JULY 4

Each person behaves after his own manner, yet only your Lord knows who chose the best path to salvation.

THE CHILDREN OF ISRAEL 17:84

Many prayers are declined because of the rank odor of a corrupt heart rising through the beautiful words. Let the words be wrong, but the meaning right. That flawed utterance is dearer to God.

Rumi, *The Life and Thought of Rumi,* p. 139

JULY 5

In truth have We revealed the Qur'an, and with truth has it come down to you. We chose you only to be the herald of glad tidings and also to give warning. Therefore We revealed the Qur'an gradually that you may recite it to humankind in stages. Thus We disclosed it in sequential revelation.

THE CHILDREN OF ISRAEL 17:105–6

A person once asked the Prophet Muhammad to pray for him. So the Prophet implored, "O Allah, kindle within his heart the light of faith, and afford him with the courage to avert earthly wiles and submit himself before Your will." When a person turns away from the world, he adheres to God, and God lavishes incredible bounty on him.

Sheikh Abdul Qadir Jillani,
Fayuz E Yazdani, p. 462

JULY 6

Say, "It is up to you to believe in the Qur'an or to deny it. Yet those who were endowed with the knowledge about its revelation,[13] fall down prostrate on their faces when it is recited before them and declare, 'Glory be to our Lord; His promise has been fulfilled.'"

THE CHILDREN OF ISRAEL 17:107–8

He that was born in the dark water of material wealth, how could he tell the freedom of open country from the dismal prison of the well? When you relinquish the ego for fear of God, the elixir of His fountain will arrive.

Rumi, *Mathnawi*, 6:3500–3501

JULY 7

Invoke Him as Allah, or invoke Him as the Beneficent. Whatever name you invoke Him by it is the same, because His are the most beautiful names. Pray neither with a loud voice nor in worship be silent, but follow a way between.

THE CHILDREN OF ISRAEL 17:110

My Lord, my desire in this world is to remember You above all other things of this world and the next and, out of all who are in that world, to be the one to meet with You alone. However, this is what I say: "Your will be done."

Rabi'a, in Rabi'a the Mystic, p. 30

JULY 8

In respect to any matter do not say, "I shall do that tomorrow," without adding, "except if Allah will." Then if you forget, remember your Lord and say, "May my Lord guide me closer to the truth."

THE CAVE 18:23–24

Relying upon the promise of "tomorrow," many people have wandered around that door, but that tomorrow never comes.

Rumi, *Mathnawi*, 1:2279

JULY 9

Recite what has been revealed to you from the Scripture of your Lord. None can ever alter His words, and you will find no refuge except Him.

THE CAVE 18:27

Adorn the Qur'an with your voices.

The Prophet Muhammad, as reported by
Al-Bar'a bin A'zib, *Al-Hadis,* 3:699

JULY 10

Those who believe and remain upright shall not
be denied the reward of their noble deeds.

THE CAVE 18:30

When you experience pain,
ask God for forgiveness.
By the command of the Creator,
it will be eliminated.
For when He decrees, pain becomes joy,
and fetters become freedom.

Rumi, *Mathnawi*, 1:836–37

JULY 11

Wealth and children are an ornament of the life
of this world. But the good deeds that endure
are better rewarded by your Lord and hold a
greater hope for your salvation.

THE CAVE 18:46

*The wealth of this world consists of treasures,
to which there are keys. But blessed is the one
whom the Almighty makes a key to the world
of good, but a lock to contain evil.*

The Prophet Muhammad, as reported by
Sahl bin Sa'ad, *Al-Hadis,* 2:731

JULY 12

Abraham said, "Peace be with you! I shall implore forgiveness of my Lord for you, for He has been gracious to me."

MARY 19:47

Hardship may dishearten at first,
but every hardship passes away.
All despair is followed by hope;
all darkness is followed by sunshine.

Rumi, *Mathnawi*, 3:2924–25

July 13

We bestowed Our mercy on them and granted them high and true renown.

MARY 19:50

When clutches of the "self" break away,
they clap their hands and break into dance
as their imperfections fade away.
The musicians within strike the tambourine,
and the seas burst into foam at their ecstasy.

Rumi, *The Life and Thought*
of Rumi, p. 105

JULY 14

He is the Lord of the heavens and the earth and all that is between them. Therefore worship Him and be steadfast in His service. For do you know any other deserving of His name?

MARY 19:65

Two groups of people seek proximity of God, those who revere Him publicly and are held in high regard by the sacred law, and those who do not display their devotion. Secure in the knowledge that God alone bestows all that is good or bad in this world, they choose Him as their companion and are delivered of want. The former because of their own need remain veiled from divine guidance, while the latter transcend through selflessness.

Abu'l-Sari Mansur bin Ammar,
The Kashf al-Mahjub, p. 127

JULY 15

Allah increases the guidance of those who remain steadfast. Good deeds that endure shall
earn you a far greater merit in the sight of your
Lord and a more promising end.

MARY 19:76

*The ways are various, but the way to Truth is
only one. Those who travel on the way of Truth
must keep themselves isolated.*

Abd al-Wahid bin Zaid,
in *Rabi'a the Mystic*, p. 10

JULY 16

All things in the heavens and on the earth shall return before the Beneficent in complete submission. Indeed He is cognizant of each one of His creatures by number. One by one shall they approach Him on the Day of Resurrection. Then those who were righteous and adhered to the true faith shall be cherished by the Merciful.

MARY 19:93–96

Do not talk ill of the dead, for they have reached the final destination to receive what they sent before them.

The Prophet Muhammad, as reported by
A'ishah bint Abi Bakr, *Al-Hadis,* 3:42

JULY 17

Behold, I am Allah. There is no God save Me. Serve Me therefore and establish worship in My remembrance. Behold the Hour is bound to come. But I prefer to keep it hidden so that every soul may be recompensed for its endeavors.

TA HA 20:14–15

The best dhikr[14] is: "There is no god but Allah"; and the best invocation: "All praise is due to Allah."

The Prophet Muhammad, as reported by Ja'bir bin Abd'Allah, *Al-Hadis,* 3:743

July 18

Our Lord is the One who gave everything its distinguishing nature and then guided it befittingly.

TA HA 20:50

Wisdom is the table, not bread or meat. Wisdom is the light, food for the soul. No nutriment can compare to the nourishment of light. Nothing can nourish the soul but light. Rid yourself of material needs and be set free. Taste the original victual, the dainty morsel of light.

Rumi, *Mathnawi*, 4:1954–57

JULY 19

He commanded the earth to spread out like a carpet for you and enabled you to trace roads therein. He showered water from the sky that enabled the growth of many kinds of vegetation to nourish you and to pasture your cattle. Herein are signs for those endowed with perception.

TA HA 20:53–54

When the mirror of the heart becomes pure and clear, impressions of the other world will become manifest. The image and the image-maker will become visible, like the carpet and the carpet-spreader.

Rumi, *Mathnawi*, 2:72–73

JULY 20

Children of Israel, I delivered you from your enemy and made a covenant with you on the right side of the holy mountain. Then I sent down the manna and quails and bade you to eat of the good things that were provided for you and warned you not to transgress, lest My wrath be incurred. For those who incur My wrath perish.

TA HA 20:80–81

Fear is a state of darkness in which the soul wanders, bewildered, seeking help, and then comes hope as a ray of light, and grace prevails.

Al-Sarraj, in *Rabi'a the Mystic*, p. 69

JULY 21

His Lord chose him [Adam], and relented toward him, and gave him guidance.

TA HA 20:122

Until the conviction in God is completely embedded in your heart, focus your attention on worldly responsibilities. When faith reaches fruition, turn toward Him in complete surrender, knowing that He it is who bestows all bounty, and He it is who takes away all.

Sheikh Abdul Qadir Jillani,
Fayuz E Yazdani, p. 165

July 22

Enjoin worship upon your people and persevere therein. Remember, We do not ask you for any provision. Instead it is We who sustain you. Blessed is the end of the righteous.

TA HA 20:132

The falcon made the king's hand his joy, and became indifferent to the search for carrion. All animals from the gnat to the elephant are of the family of God and depend on Him for sustenance. What a sustainer is God!

Rumi, *Mathnawi*, 1:2294–95

JULY 23

He said, "My Lord is aware of every word uttered in the heaven and the earth. He hears all, knows all."

THE PROPHETS 21:4

Do away with superfluous speech, and sacrifice what you hold dear, that His grace may utter praise of you and the heaven be envious of your exalted estate.

Rumi, *Mathnawi*, 3:2728–29

JULY 24

We hurl truth against falsehood, until truth triumphs and falsehood is annihilated. Woe be to you, for all the falsehoods that you ascribe to Him.

THE PROPHETS 21:18

Give up what appears to be doubtful for what is certain. Truth brings peace of mind, and deception doubt.

The Prophet Muhammad, as reported by Hasan bin 'Ali, *Al-Hadis*, 1:464

JULY 25

All creatures in the heavens and on the earth belong to Him. Even those who dwell in His presence are not too proud to serve Him, nor are they ever wearied.

When God's decree becomes your pleasure,
you become a willing slave,
not because of burdening yourself,
not on account of recompense,
but by virtue of the nature now so pure
that wherever divine edict may take you,
living and dying appear the same.
You live for God, not for riches;
you die for God, not from fear or pain.

Rumi, *Mathnawi*, 3:1906–7, 1909–10

July 26

We set the earth with stabilizing mountains, lest it shake with the weight of creation, and We placed therein ravines as pathways for them to pass through that they may find their way.

THE PROPHETS 21:31

The face of David shone with His glory,
and the mountains sang His praise.
The mountains sang along with David;
both elated in praising the King.
He hears the melody of the pure-spirited,
every moment, every place.

Rumi, *Mathnawi*, 3:4268–69, 4276

JULY 27

Job cried unto his Lord: "Adversity has afflicted me, but You are the Most Merciful of all those who show mercy." Then We heard his prayer and removed his affliction, and restored to him his family and blessed him with new offspring, doubling the number thereof. This was a benediction from Us and a reminder to all those who worship us."

The Prophets 21:83–84

When a starved, impoverished person conceals his needs from others, then know that the Almighty Lord will provide for him through His infinite bounty.

The Prophet Muhammad, as reported by
Abd'Allah ibn Abbas, *Al-Hadis,* 1:279

JULY 28

Jonah went off in anger and deemed that We had no power over him! But then he cried out in darkness, saying, "There is no God save You. Glory be to You! Indeed I was in the wrong." Then We heard his prayer and saved him from his anguish. Thus We save the believers.

THE PROPHETS 21:87–88

Fear is like a candle whose flame helps a person distinguish goodness from evil; and fear of God allows a person to turn away from evil. Those who fear mere creatures flee from them; but those who fear God flee to Him.

Rabiʿa, in *Rabiʿa the Mystic*, p. 67

JULY 29

Whoever performs good deeds and has faith, his endeavor shall not be rejected. We record everything for him.

THE PROPHETS 21:94

During prayer I give myself over to the Lord
and delight myself in zealous worship.
The window of my soul opens wide
and the Book of God comes to view
To fill my house with grace and light.

Rumi, *Mathnawi*, 3:2401–3

JULY 30

It was written in the Scripture (Torah) before it was written in the Psalms, "The righteous shall inherit the earth." This is a plain message for the devout.

THE PROPHETS 21:105–6

He sprang from his sleep to behold the blind man reading from the Qur'an. "O you with no eyes, how can you see those lines?"

The blind man replied, "I begged my Lord, crying, 'O You who help those who seek, restore my sight that I may read the Book of Life.' My Lord replied, 'O man of devotion, whose hope am I, when you want to read this Book of Mine, you shall have sight at that time.' So the King restored my eyes, like a lamp till the end of night."

Rumi, *Mathnawi*, 3:1835, 1856–71

JULY 31

Those who were guided to gentle speech, indeed they were guided onto the path of the Glorious One.

THE PILGRIMAGE 22:24

Speech is a great blessing conferred on man by God, thereby distinguishing him from all other creatures. But speech like wine intoxicates the mind. Thus the Prophet said: "He who keeps silent shall be saved." For in silence are concealed many spiritual blessings and in speech many evils.

Al-Hujwiri, *The Kashf al-Mahjub*, p. 355

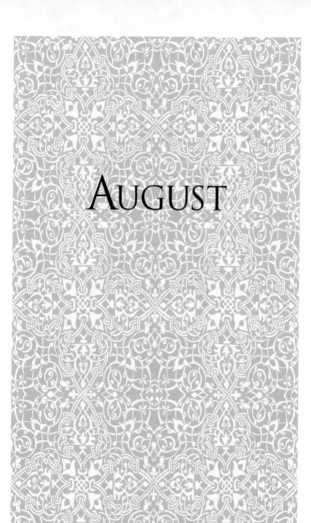

AUGUST

AUGUST 1

It is not the flesh of the sacrificial animals
or their blood that reaches Allah. It is your
piety that reaches Him. He has thus made them
subject to you that you may glorify Him for
guiding you on the right path. Give the good
news to all the righteous.

THE PILGRIMAGE 22:37

Renunciation of the world does not constitute
wearing coarse clothes and eating stale bread.
Real renunciation lies in curbing desires.

Sufyan Thawri, *Al-Hadis*, 1:434

AUGUST 2

Verily! Allah will defend those who are true. Allah does not love the treacherous and the ungrateful.

THE PILGRIMAGE 22:38

Once the Prophet was asked, "Who are the chosen people of God?"

He replied, "The truthful and the pure-hearted."

"O Prophet of Allah," they said, "truthful we understand, but who are the pure-hearted?"

"Those who neither fall into sin, nor transgress, who neither deceive nor bear malice. Such are the pure of heart."

Reported by Abd'Allah bin Amr,
Al-Hadis, 1:466

AUGUST 3

Do you not see how Allah sends down water from the sky and the earth becomes clothed in green? Only Allah understands the subtle mysteries. Allah is All-Aware.

THE PILGRIMAGE 22:63

Demolish this house that a hundred more may be built. Do not be afraid that treasure lies beneath this house. A thousand houses more shall you build with just one treasure in hand. This house is destined to fall to ruin. That treasure is bound to be unearthed, but then that treasure will not be yours.

Rumi, *Mathnawi*, 4:2540–44

AUGUST 4

You who believe! Bow down and prostrate yourselves. Worship your Lord and remain righteous that you may prosper.

THE PILGRIMAGE 22:77

When he prostrated himself before Allah, the Prophet used to say, "O Allah! Forgive me my sins, the foremost of the sins and last of the sins, minor sins and grave sins, those I hide and those I lay open."

Reported by Abu Hurairah,
Al-Hadis, 3:286

AUGUST 5

Fortunate are the believers who humble themselves in their prayers, who avoid vain talk, and
who give in charity.

THE BELIEVERS 23:1–4

Behold the words of the Qur'an:
"We are closer to you than you are yourself."
Comprehend your relationship with God!
He is closer to us than our own selves.
Yet through ignorance we search for Him
Wandering from door to door.

A Sufi poem, in *Islamic Sufism,* p. 99

August 6

Apostles enjoy all things good and pure and remain righteous. For I am well aware of what you do. Verily this brotherhood of yours is a single brotherhood, and I am your Lord. So remain observant to Me.

THE BELIEVERS 23:51–52

Your power comes from the power of God,
not from the veins or the beating heart.
The power of the saints comes from God,
not from feasts and trays of provisions.
They were created from the light
that transcends the angel and the Spirit alike.

Rumi, *Mathnawi*, 3:3, 7–8

AUGUST 7

We do not burden any soul beyond its limits.
With Us lies a record that reveals the truth, and
no one will ever be wronged.

THE BELIEVERS 23:62

Shed tears when you are aggrieved.
Your grief will heal those in grief.
Be steadfast and awaken, fast regularly, starve!
Starvation is one of the labors of surrender.

Sha'wana, in *Rabi'a the Mystic*, p. 146

AUGUST 8

Repel evil with good. We are aware of all their slanders. So implore Allah and say, "My Lord! I seek refuge in You from the suggestions of the evil ones."

THE BELIEVERS 23:96

Bereft of life, bereft of knowledge,
bereft of power and will,
how shall I describe my state?
For I do not exist; only He exists.
I am deaf; the hearer is He.
I am blind; the seer is He.
I am mute; the orator is He.
I do not exist; only He exists.

Shah Kamal, in *Islamic Sufism*, p. 101

AUGUST 9

Among My servants were those who used to entreat, "Our Lord! We believe. Therefore forgive us and have mercy on us, for You indeed are the Most Merciful of those who show mercy." But you chose to make a laughing stock of them to a point that you forgot to remember Me and continued scoffing at them. Behold, today I reward them for their perseverance; indeed they have triumphed.

THE BELIEVERS 23:109–11

Humbly do I implore You, keep me in Your divine grace, and deprive me not of peace. Save me from sudden misfortunes; deliver me and sustain me. May I never displease You, my Lord.

Cited in the prayer book
Al-Hizbul-A'zam, p. 25 (14)

AUGUST 10

Allah is the Light of the heavens and the earth.
His light is like a lamp enclosed within a glass
in a niche. The glass is like a brilliant star kin-
dled from a blessed olive tree neither of the
East nor of the West, whose very oil is luminous, though no fire has touched it. Light upon
light, Allah guides to His light whom He will.
He propounds parables to humankind since He
alone has complete knowledge of all things.

LIGHT 24:35

The light of God is an ornament of wisdom.
That is the meaning of "light upon light."
The light of reason draws toward the earth.
The light of God carries you aloft.
Things of reason are of the lower world.
The light of God is an ocean,
reason merely a dewdrop.

Rumi, *Mathnawi*, 2:1293–95

AUGUST 11

Have you not seen that all in the heavens and on the earth praise Allah, even the birds as they wing their flight? Each one knows its own way of worship and praise. Allah is aware of all that they do.

LIGHT 24:41

I commence with the name of Allah. When His name is invoked, all evil in the heavens and on the earth is rendered powerless. He hears all and knows all.

Cited in the collection
Munajat E Maqbool, p. 142

AUGUST 12

Indeed We sent down revelations and explained them. Then Allah guides whom He will onto a straight path.

LIGHT 24:46

When the Prophet addressed his people, he repeated each sentence three times, so that everyone present could understand.

Reported by Anas bin Malik,
Al-Hadis, 1:370

AUGUST 13

Establish worship, give in charity, and obey the messenger that you may find mercy.

LIGHT 24:56

Every morning two angels come down from the Heaven. One says, "O Allah! Reward all those who give in Your cause," while the other says, "O Allah! Uproot every miser who withholds."

The Prophet Muhammad, as reported by Abu Hurairah, *Al-Hadis,* 2:24

AUGUST 14

It is He who created man from water and appointed for him kindred by blood and kindred by marriage; your Lord is ever powerful.

THE CRITERION 25:54

Lord, bless us with amiable companions and children that may be a source of delight to our eyes. Allow us to be of the devout.

Cited in the prayer book
Al-Hizbul-A'zam, p. 6 (42)

AUGUST 15

Have faith in the Ever-Living, who dies not,
and celebrate His praise. He is well aware of
all His servants' sins.

THE CRITERION 25:58

*Knowledge has two wings. Conjecture is one
wing. Conjecture alone is lacking and cuts
short the flight. The one-winged bird continues
to struggle, hoping to reach the nest somehow
with one wing. And then wisdom shows his
shining face. Delivered from conjecture, the
bird now spreads both wings (and soars once
again).*

Rumi, *The Life and Thought
of Rumi*, p. 153

August 16

He created the heavens and the earth and all
that exists between them in six days. Then
He mounted the glorious Throne. Allah is the
Most Gracious. Ask those who have knowledge
concerning Him!

The Criterion 25:59

Lord, illumine my heart with your light,
my eyes with your effulgence,
my ears with your radiance.
Your light to my right, light to my left,
light above, light below,
light before me, light behind me.
Allow your light to surround me, Lord.

The Prophet Muhammad, as reported by
Abd'Allah ibn Abbas,
Sahih al-Bukhari, p. 974

AUGUST 17

Blessed is He who decked the heavens with constellations of stars and placed therein a blazing lamp, the sun and a moon that reflects light. It is He who caused the night and the day to succeed one another. In all these are signs for the mindful who are grateful.

THE CRITERION 25:61–62

Indeed the whole world is imagination.
Only He is the real in Reality.
Whoever understands this
knows the secrets of the spiritual path.

Ibn 'Arabi, in *Masters of the Path*, p. 56

AUGUST 18

The faithful servants of the Beneficent walk upon the earth modestly, and when the ignorant address them, they say: "Peace!" They spend the night standing and prostrating before their Lord and say, "Lord, avert from us the doom of Hell, for its torment is everlasting. It is an evil resting place, a wretched abode indeed."

THE CRITERION 25:63–64

The saints are My children in exile,
torn away from My dominion and glory.
Despised and alone they endure their trials;
in secret I am their intimate friend.

Rumi, *Mathnawi*, 3:82–83

AUGUST 19

Have they not seen the earth, how We cause every beneficial plant to grow therein?

THE POETS 26:7

When one of you plants a tree, the fruits of which all creatures enjoy, let it be written as charity.

The Prophet Muhammad, as reported by Anas bin Malik, *Al-Hadis,* 1:328

AUGUST 20

When the two hosts[15] saw each other, the people of Moses said, "We are indeed overtaken." Moses said, "By no means! My Lord is with me, and He will guide me."

THE POETS 26:61–62

Why should I grieve because of a thorn? Once it had made laughter known to me. Whatever you lost through the stroke of destiny, know it was to save you from adversity. One small affliction keeps off greater afflictions; one small loss prevents greater losses.

Rumi, Mathnawi, 3:3259–60, 3265

AUGUST 21

He created me and guides me, He feeds me and
nourishes me, and when I am sick, it is He who
restores me to health. He will cause me to die
and then will bring me back to life, and, I hope
with all sincerity, He will forgive me my sins on
the Day of Judgment.

THE POETS 26:78–82

*When a person calls upon the ailing, an angel
proclaims, "Blessed be your journey through
life, and Paradise be your final abode."*

The Prophet Muhammad, as reported by
Abu Hurairah, *Al-Hadis,* 1:286

AUGUST 22

My Lord! Bestow wisdom upon me, and admit me amid the righteous. Allow me to be worthy of praise in the generations to come, and place me among the heirs of the Gardens of bliss.

THE POETS 26:83–85

When you proclaim immanence alone you limit God. When you assert devotion alone you confine Him. But when you maintain both side by side, you follow the right path, and gain both inner merit and command of gnosis.

Ibn 'Arabi, in *Islamic Sufism*,
pp. 100–101

AUGUST 23

He [Noah] said, "My Lord! My own people have rejected me. Therefore judge between us, and deliver me and those believers who are with me." So We saved him and those with him in a laden ark.

THE POETS 26:117–19

Persevere, have faith in His benevolence.
Through afflictions God only tests your faith;
He is completely aware of your condition.
Have patience and wait for the divine decree.
Do not become like the foolish laborer
who is removed from the king's palace
for demanding his wages ahead of time.

Sheikh Abdul Qadir Jillani,
Fayuz E Yazdani, p. 363

AUGUST 24

Do not withhold goods justly due to others, nor act corruptly on the earth, spreading evil. Remain conscious of Him who created you and the numerous generations before you.

THE POETS 26:183–184

The false promises of a merchant may persuade a buyer into purchasing his (faulty) goods; but these will be deprived of Allah's blessings.

The Prophet Muhammad, as reported by Abu Hurairah, *Sahih al-Bukhari*, p. 469

August 25

Warn your nearest kinsfolk, and show kindness to those who follow you. But if they disobey you, say, "I am not accountable for what you do."

THE POETS 26:214–16

Take to compassion and abstain from oppression and obscenity. Compassion is grace and the lack of it a disgrace.

The Prophet Muhammad, as reported by
A'ishah bint Abi Bakr, *Al-Hadis,* 1:333

AUGUST 26

Place all your confidence in the Almighty, the
All-Merciful, who observes you when you
stand up to pray, and also when you walk
among the worshipers. He, only He, hears and
knows all things.

THE POETS 26:217–20

*When the Imam[16] says, "Allah hears those
who praise Him," respond with, "Yours is the
praise, our Lord." When the angels hear this,
they declare, "He has been absolved of his
sins."*

The Prophet Muhammad, as reported by
Abu Hurairah, *Al-Hadis,* 3:280

AUGUST 27

We gave knowledge to David and Solomon, who said, "Praise be to Allah, who has exalted us above so many of His believing servants."

THE ANT 27:15

Do not become the candle that gives light to others but itself remains in darkness. Do not follow the desires of your lower self. Should the Lord wish, He Himself will pick you out and prompt you to be a source of guidance. He Himself shall endow you with the inner strength to endure the changes of fortune and will instill within you infinite wisdom.

Sheikh Abdul Qadir Jillani,
Fayuz E Yazdani, p. 301

August 28

Solomon laughed at her [the ant's] speech and said, "My Lord, inspire me to be thankful for the favor that You bestowed upon me and my parents by allowing me to do good works pleasing to You. Bestow upon me Your loving kindness and admit me among Your righteous servants."

THE ANT 27:19

O Beloved of hearts, I beseech only You.
Have pity this day on those who turn to You.
My Hope, my Rest, my Delight,
this heart can love none other but You.

Rabi'a, in *Rabi'a the Mystic*, p. 55

August 29

Who responds to the distressed when they cry out to Him and who removes their affliction? Did He not make you the inheritors of the earth? Could there then be another God beside Allah? Little do you reflect!

THE ANT 27:62

Sufficient is our Lord for us. He is the greatest of all helpers; we depend upon Him alone.

Cited in the collection
Munajat E Maqbool, p. 160

AUGUST 30

Is it not He who guides you in the darkness of the land and the sea and sends the winds as heralds of His mercy? Then is there another God besides Allah? Exalted be Allah above all that they associate with Him.

THE ANT 27:63

Winds are the heralds of Allah's mercy, though they bear both compassion and chastisement. So implore Allah for their aid, and seek refuge in Him from their destructive power.

The Prophet Muhammad, as reported by
Abu Hurairah, Al-Hadis, 3:506

AUGUST 31

So We restored him [Moses] to his mother that she might be comforted and not grieve, that she might know that the promise of Allah is true. But most of them know not. And when he reached maturity and had grown to manhood, We endowed him with knowledge and wisdom. Thus do We reward the good.

THE STORY 28:13–14

Allah exalted two kinds of people above others: those who spend in the cause of the Truth, and the judicious who impart their wisdom to others.

The Prophet Muhammad, as reported by Nayeem bin Mas'ud, *Al-Hadis*, 1:347

SEPTEMBER

SEPTEMBER 1

He[17] said, "My Lord! I have wronged my soul, so forgive me," and Allah forgave him. For He is the Most Forgiving, the Beneficent.

THE STORY 28:16

Do not deem yourself prudent, for as long as you are attached to the world, you have neither prudence nor sense. Turn to God and seek forgiveness if you wish to prevail. Listen to your heart and not your ego. Your ego prompts you to boast of vain assertions to obtain the glory of this world. Turn away from vanity and seek Him in the recesses of your heart and soul. Show patience in adversity and be content in His will that you may attain proximity to God.

Sheikh Abdul Qadir Jillani,
Fayuz E Yazdani, p. 216

SEPTEMBER 2

My Lord! For the grace that You have bestowed upon me, I shall never support the wrongdoers.

THE STORY 27:17

Lord, forgive us our transgressions.
Help us remain steadfast.
We seek Your support against the transgressors.

Cited in the prayer book
Al-Hizbul-A'zam, p. 4 (14)

September 3

So he [Moses] watered their flock for them. Then he retired into the shade and said, "My Lord, I stand in desperate need of whatever blessings You may send down for me."

THE STORY 28:24

Are you oblivious of the bounty of God who invites you to come yonder? The whole world of six directions is brimming with His bounty. Wherever you turn, His munificence is manifest.

Rumi, *Mathnawi*, 3:3107–8

SEPTEMBER 4

We shall strengthen your arm with the arm of
your brother, and We will give you [Moses and
Aaron] both power, so that they will not be
able to harm you because of Our signs. Go
forth, both of you, and those who follow you
shall surely be victorious.

THE STORY 28:35

O Allah! You are my helping hand, my savior.
I get all my strength from You.
I strike with Your help,
and only with Your help do I combat.

The Prophet Muhammad, as reported by
Anas bin Malik, *Al-Hadis,* 3:783

SEPTEMBER 5

When they hear idle chatter they withdraw from it and say, "We have our deeds and you have yours. Peace be with you. We do not seek the ignorant."

THE STORY 28:55

Observe how the life of this world deceives those around you. It lures them into the traps of vanity, wealth, and fame, and exalts them above others. This splendor blinds them, and they are lost forever in illusion. But then in one instant, life deals the blow of death, and all is gone, and with the Beguiler it stands laughing at their sad end. So overcome your egos that you may be saved from the snares that devoured kings and paupers alike.

Sheikh Abdul Qadir Jillani,
Fayuz E Yazdani, p. 128

SEPTEMBER 6

You will not be able to guide everyone you love, for Allah guides whom He will. He knows best who are rightly guided.

THE STORY 28:56

Knowledge is of three kinds: from God, with God, of God. Knowledge of God is disclosed to all prophets and saints; it is a divine guidance and cannot be acquired. Knowledge from God is the sacred law made obligatory upon us. Knowledge with God is the knowledge of the paths and stations and the development of saints.

Al-Hujwiri, *The Kashf al-Mahjub*, p. 16

SEPTEMBER 7

Those who repent, accept the true faith, and remain steadfast shall reside among those who have achieved salvation.

THE STORY 28:67

Though all the children of Adam are marred by sin, the finest of the sinners are those who repent constantly.

The Prophet Muhammad, as reported by Anas bin Malik, *Al-Hadis,* 3:760

SEPTEMBER 8

Seek the abode of the hereafter by means of the wealth that Allah has bestowed upon you, yet do not neglect your own share in this world. Be kind to others, as Allah has been kind to you, and do not spread corruption on the earth, for Allah does not love the wrongdoers.

THE STORY 28:77

Liberate yourself from the fetters of the ego and surrender yourself before God. Let the Lord be your shepherd, allow Him to attend to all your cares, and do not allow temptations to entice you. Aspirations of this world are the cause of all concern. Aspire to God and obtain freedom.

Sheikh Abdul Qadir Jillani,
Futhul Ghaib, p. 25

SEPTEMBER 9

As for those who believe and do good works,
We shall remit their evil deeds and reward them
according to the noblest of their deeds.

THE SPIDER 29:7

*Allah shall pardon all those who abstain from
corruption, especially when they are inclined
toward it.*

Abu Hurairah, *Al-Hadis*, 3:131

SEPTEMBER 10

Some claim to have faith in Allah, yet when they are made to suffer in His cause, they confuse the persecution of men for Allah's wrath. Yet when Allah makes you victorious they say, "We were on your side all the while." Is Allah not aware of what is in the hearts of his creatures? Indeed He knows those who believe, and without doubt He knows the hypocrites.

THE SPIDER 29:10–11

Practice patience; it is the essence of praise.
Have patience, for that is true worship.
No other worship is worth as much.
Have patience; patience is the key to all relief.

Rumi, *Mathnawi*, 2:3145–46

SEPTEMBER 11

Sufficient is Allah as witness between you and me. He has knowledge of all that dwells in the heavens and on the earth. Those who believe in vainglory and renounce Allah shall be among the losers.

THE SPIDER 29:52

Whenever a transgressor is praised, the Almighty Allah becomes enraged, and the Throne shudders in dismay.

The Prophet Muhammad, as reported by
Anas bin Malik, Al-Hadis, 1:469

SEPTEMBER 12

Those who believe and do good works shall dwell forever in the lofty mansions of Paradise underneath which the rivers flow. There they shall live forever. What a glorious reward for the righteous.

THE SPIDER 29:58

I am a bridge across the ocean for my devotee,
but become a dragon for the Pharaoh.
Rejoice, O lovers, entreat God.
The same door has been opened again.
The fruit is beckoning, "Eat of me."
The water of life is inviting, "Drink of me."

Rumi, *Mathnawi*, 4:1070, 1082, 1104

SEPTEMBER 13

There are numerous animals that cannot sustain themselves. Allah provides for them, as He provides for you. He hears all and knows all.

THE SPIDER 29:60

Strengthen me, my Lord,
for I am overcome with feebleness.
Ennoble me once more,
for I have been cast down.
Sustain me, Lord,
for I am impoverished.

Cited in the prayer book
Al-Hizbul-A'zam, p. 30 (54)

September 14

As for those who strive for Us, We will most certainly guide them onto Our paths. Indeed Allah is with the righteous.

THE SPIDER 29:69

Those who glorified Allah both in open and in secret will be the foremost to enter Paradise on the Day of Resurrection.

The Prophet Muhammad, as reported by Abd'Allah ibn Abbas, *Al-Hadis*, 3:748

SEPTEMBER 15

And among His numerous signs is that He created mates for you from among yourselves, that you might find peace with them, and He ordained love and mercy between you. Indeed there are signs in this for those who reflect.

THE ROMANS 30:21

The finest of the believers conduct themselves with honorable bearing. And the finest of the finest are those who treat their mates with affection.

The Prophet Muhammad, as reported by
Abu Hurairah, *Al-Hadis,* 1:213

SEPTEMBER 16

Do they not see that it is Allah who bestows abundant sustenance, and that only He provides sparingly to whom He pleases? There are indeed signs in this for those who believe. So give in alms to the near of kin, to the needy, and to the wayfarer. That is the best for those who strive to please Allah, for they shall certainly prosper.

THE ROMANS 30:37–38

Children of Adam! Distribute your surplus wealth in the name of Allah; it will earn you more merit. Do not hold it back. You must not be remembered for miserliness, so begin with those closest to you.

The Prophet Muhammad, as reported by
Abu Umamah, *Al-Hadis,* 2:25

SEPTEMBER 17

My son, establish worship, enjoin kindness, and forbid iniquity. Endure patiently through every adversity; indeed that requires tremendous courage.

LUQMAN 31:17

Bitter is made sweet through love;
copper becomes gold through love.
Through love dregs become clear;
love heals all pain.
Through love the king becomes slave;
love brings the dead to life.

Rumi, *Mathnawi*, 2:1529–30

SEPTEMBER 18

Do not treat people with contempt, nor walk insolently on the earth. Allah does not love the arrogant or the self-conceited boaster. Be modest in your bearing and subdue your voice, for the most unpleasant of voices is the braying of the ass.

LUQMAN 31:18–19

Woe to you, O baser self! How great your incredulity, how dreadful your ignorance, how immense your boldness for sin. How long will you break your promises? What keeps you engaged in the pursuits of the world? Will you never leave this world? Look upon those who rest in graves, how they amassed wealth, how they built lofty buildings. How high must their hopes be? But in vain. Their wealth has vanished, the buildings are rubble. Why do you not learn from these things?

Al-Ghazzali, *Ihya Ulum Id-Din*,
4:428–29

SEPTEMBER 19

Whoever surrenders his purpose to Allah and remains virtuous, he indeed has grasped the most dependable handle. In the end all things will return to Allah.

LUQMAN 31:22

O All-Knowing, you opened my heart to the way of supplication. Yearning for Your love is glorious and grand; lust for other love is disgraceful and corrupt. Your divine court is the infinite plane. I leave behind the throne of honor, for the real throne of honor is Your way.

Rumi, *Mathnawi*, 3:1952, 1955–56, 1961

SEPTEMBER 20

If all the trees on the earth were pens, and
the sea, replenished with seven more seas, were
ink, the words of Allah would still not be ex-
hausted. Indeed Allah is the Almighty, the Wise.

LUQMAN 31:27

*Because of your humility God granted you the
gift of insight. Go toward the peach tree, which
has sprung to life. It has become lush green by
the command "Be!" Beneath its shade all your
needs will be fulfilled. Such is divine alchemy
that the crooked become straight. As God revealed, "Its roots are firm in the earth, its
branches in the sky."*

Rumi, *Mathnawi*, 4:3566–74

SEPTEMBER 21

Those who truly believe Our revelations fall down prostrate and celebrate the praise of their Lord when they are reminded of them; and such are not contemptuous.

THE PROSTRATION 32:15

Lord, have mercy on our souls and allow us to follow Your commandments. O Most Compassionate One, do not allow our hearts to err after being guided aright.

Cited in the prayer book
Al-Hizbul-A'zam, p. 3 (8)

September 22

Only those believe in Our revelations who forsake their beds to implore their Lord in fear and hope and give in alms of what We have bestowed on them. Mortals can never imagine what blissful delights have been kept hidden from them as a reward for all their hard work.

THE PROSTRATION 32:15–16

The Almighty Allah says: "For the righteous I have prepared that which no eyes have envisioned and no hearts conceived. Search all you want, no living soul shall ever perceive what ultimate bliss is concealed from them."

The Prophet Muhammad, as reported by
Abu Hurairah, *Al-Hadis,* 4:161

SEPTEMBER 23

O Prophet, remain conscious of Allah and do not give in to the unbelievers or the hypocrites. Remember that Allah is Knowing and Discerning. Follow, therefore, what has been revealed to you by your Lord, who is aware of all that you do. (Have faith in Allah;) sufficient is He as your Trustee.

THE CLANS 33:1–3

During times of uncertainty the Prophet used to entreat, "Allah, there is no God but Allah, the Exalted, the Forbearing, Lord of the tremendous Throne, Lord of the heavens and the earth."

Reported by Abd'Allah ibn Abbas,
Al-Hadis, 3:775

SEPTEMBER 24

Allah shall reward the truthful for standing by their word and may punish the hypocrites if that be His will or may relent toward them should they repent, for Allah is the Most Forgiving, Merciful.

THE CLANS 33:24

Forgive us, our Lord. Overlook our transgressions and remit from us our evil deeds. Condemn us not for our corruption; save us from public scorn. O Merciful, You Yourself decreed, "I alone and no other accept repentance of My servants and remit from them their evil deeds." So absolve us of our sins, O Benevolent Lord.

Sheikh Abdul Qadir Jillani,
Fayuz E Yazdani, p. 322

SEPTEMBER 25

Indeed, all men and women who surrender themselves to Allah and are devout and trustworthy, who persevere through adversity and are humble and charitable, who fast and are ever mindful of their chastity, all men and women who remember Allah unceasingly shall be exonerated and blessed with an immense reward.

THE CLANS 33:35

You shall be able to identify the true believers by their kindness and compassion. They are like one body: when one limb hurts, the entire body responds with restlessness and fever.

The Prophet Muhammad, as reported by
Nu'man bin Bashir, *Al-Hadis*, 1:291

SEPTEMBER 26

Believers remember Allah steadfastly and glorify Him morning and evening. For it is He who sends blessings on you as do His angels, that He may lead you from darkness to light. Allah is most beneficent to the devoted.

THE CLANS 33:41–43

Patience comes in three stages: first, one learns not to follow the baser self; second, one learns to content oneself with one's fate; finally, one surrenders oneself to the Master's will and discovers within love and compassion, the greatest of all achievements.

Al-Ghazzali, *Ihya Ulum Id-Din,* 4:72

SEPTEMBER 27

On the day they meet their Lord, they shall be welcomed by the salutation "Peace!" An illustrious reward has been prepared for them. O Prophet, indeed We have sent you as a witness and a bearer of good tidings and also to warn humankind and to invite them to Allah by His leave and guide them like the beacon that spreads light. Give the believers good tidings that a great bounty awaits them.

THE CLANS 33:44–47

Renunciation of the world is followed by peace; its desire brings sorrow. Restrain your desires, discipline your self, and do not allow anyone to oppress your soul.

Rabi'a, in *Rabi'a the Mystic*, p. 11

SEPTEMBER 28

Indeed Allah and His angels shower blessings
on the Prophet. Then you who believe, bless
him, and salute him with all respect.

THE CLANS 33:56

Glorified by heaven, O radiant Sun, illumine
the earth forever and more that the hearts of its
inhabitants unite and ascend and become one
with the exalted Divine.

Rumi, *Mathnawi*, 4:3827–28

SEPTEMBER 29

Believers, remain mindful of Allah and always tell the truth. He will bless you with forthrightness and absolve you of your sins. Those who adhere to Allah and His messenger shall indeed have achieved a signal victory.

THE CLANS 33:70–71

God calls Himself "Seeing" so that His ever-watching eye may scare you away from sinning. Whether the breeze be cold or hot, the Cognizant is aware, not absent, O infirm man.

Rumi, *Mathnawi*, 4:215, 234

SEPTEMBER 30

Say, "You shall not be held accountable for our transgressions, nor shall we be responsible for what you have done. Our Lord will gather us all together in the end. Then He will decide between us with truth and justice, for He is the Judge who perceives all."

SABA 34:25–26

Sovereigns and slaves, oppressors and mediators, hypocrites and the truthful, this world is passing, but the hereafter infinite. Strive therefore for the Lord alone. Attain to piety and purify your hearts. Save yourselves; do not be held back from divine mercy. The path of adoration may render the body weak and fill the heart with sorrow, but all sorrow departs the instant He touches the heart, awakening it to an abounding freedom.

Sheikh Abdul Qadir Jillani,
Fayuz E Yazdani, pp. 293–94

OCTOBER

OCTOBER 1

The Truth has come; falsehood has vanished and will not return. Then tell them, "If I have gone astray, then it is to my own disadvantage, and if I am rightly guided, it is because of what my Lord has revealed to me. He hears everything and is always near."

SABA 34:49–50

Flee to the shelter of God's grace. He showers our souls with His grace. When He provides shelter, how can you lack shelter? Fear not; water and fire will become your army. Did the sea not help Noah and Moses? Did it not seek vengeance upon their foes? Was not the fire a fortress for Abraham? Did it not raise the smoke of despair in the heart of Nimrod?

Rumi, *Mathnawi*, 1:1839–42

OCTOBER 2

Praise be to Allah, the Creator of the heavens
and the earth, who appointed the angels with
two, three, and four wings as His messengers.
He may multiply what He wills, for He has
power over all things. Once the gates of His
mercy have opened, none can withhold it, but
should He decide to withhold it, none has the
power to release it thereafter. Allah is the Most
Powerful and Wise.

THE ANGELS 35:1–2

*When Ahmad passed beyond the lote tree at
the boundary of Paradise, the Angel's frontier,
he said, "O Gabriel, come fly with me." But
Gabriel replied, "I cannot escort you. My wings
beyond that point will be consumed. But the
station of the pure before the Most Pure is
nothing short of wonderment."*

Rumi, *Mathnawi*, 4:3801–2, 3804–5

OCTOBER 3

Humankind! The promise of Allah is true. So do not let the life of this world beguile you, nor let the Deceiver deceive you regarding Allah. Beware, the devil is your enemy; therefore treat him as an enemy. He calls upon his followers only so that they become dwellers of the Fire.

THE ANGELS 35:5–6

Once a person said to a dervish, "All I ask for is a small dwelling in Paradise."

The dervish replied, "If you displayed the same contentment with what you already have in this world, you would have found ultimate bliss."

Sheikh Abdul Qadir Jillani,
Fayuz E Yazdani, p. 517

OCTOBER 4

No soul shall bear the burden of another, even if one overcome by his impediment pleads to be relieved of his load. None, even his kin, shall come to the aid of the other. You can warn only those who establish worship and stand in awe of their Lord, though they cannot perceive Him. Those who grow in uprightness grow only for themselves and may not by their merit redeem others. Unto Allah shall all things return.

THE ANGELS 35:18

When a believer gives in to temptation, a black stain appears on his heart. If he repents and asks for forgiveness, that stain disappears. But if he continues to transgress, the stain continues to grow until it blackens the entire heart. That stain is the rust the Lord Almighty refers to: "Nay, rust has fallen upon their hearts for what they have earned."

The Prophet Muhammad, as reported by Abu Hurairah, *Al-Hadis,* 3:760

OCTOBER 5

Praise be to Allah, who made sorrow depart from us. Certainly our Lord is forgiving and bountiful. By His grace He has allowed us to dwell in the eternal mansion where neither toil nor weariness shall ever again afflict us.

THE ANGELS 35:34–35

Even before accomplishing enlightenment a person knows that everything attests to the existence of God. But these virtuous feelings of innocence disappear as he begins to mingle with corrupt society, because worldly affairs hinder him from swimming in the vast ocean of insight.

Al-Ghazzali, *Ihya Ulum Id-Din,* 4:314

OCTOBER 6

Then a man came running from the farthest part of the city and cried, "My people, follow the messengers who are rightly guided and do not ask of any reward from you. Why should I not worship Him who brought me into being and unto whom all of you shall return? Worship other gods than the Merciful? Why, if the Lord wishes to harm me, no one will be able to save me or intercede on my behalf; and if I do worship another I would indeed be lost in grave wrong. Behold, I believe in the Lord most high." And he was granted Paradise. At that he declared, "If only my people knew, the Lord has pardoned me and placed me among the honored ones."

YA SIN 36:20–27

Like the corn fields that yield before the ferocious winds, the believers endure trials with fortitude. The hypocrites like the cypress trees stand arrogantly until they are knocked down.

The Prophet Muhammad, as reported by
Abu Hurairah, *Al-Hadis,* 1:122

OCTOBER 7

Glory be to Him who created everything in pairs: plants, human beings, and even entities they have no knowledge of. Of the many, one sign is the night. We strip it of the light of day, and abject darkness surrounds everything. The sun hastens to its resting place, its course determined by the Mighty, the All-Knowing Lord. Also ordained by the Almighty Lord are the phases of the moon, which decreases daily until it looks like a bent and shriveled palm stalk. Neither can the sun overtake the moon, nor night outstrip the day. Both float in orbits of their own.

YA SIN 36:36–40

I am a burning candle;
You are the morning light.
If I do not see You, I burn;
if I see You, I vanish.
This is my condition
in separation and closeness.
I can bear neither separation nor proximity.

A Sufi poem, in *Islamic Sufism*, p. 91

OCTOBER 8

Do not be grieved by what they say. We have
full knowledge of what they conceal and what
they do openly. Is man not aware that We
created him from a worthless drop of sperm?
Behold, he is still an open foe.

YA SIN 36:76

*God said, "Do not take offense at their
ridicule, for they are not your followers. Your
true friends hide behind the divine bounty, and
entreat for you steadily. In good health all of
them are your friends, but in the hour of pain
all depart. God is your only friend."*

Rumi, *Mathnawi*, 5:3199, 3202, 3206

OCTOBER 9

He created the heavens and the earth. Is He then not able to create the likes [of those who have died]? Certainly He is! For He is the Supreme Creator who holds all knowledge. When He intends a thing, His only command is "Be!" and it is. Glory be to Him in whose hands rests the dominion over all things. To Him shall all be brought back.

YA SIN 36:80–82

Your pleas shall be answered, but wait patiently for the Lord to respond. Do not lose hope and begin to complain, "I beseeched the Lord, but He never responded."

The Prophet Muhammad, as reported by
Abu Hurairah,
Sahih al-Bukhari, p. 975 (2078)

OCTOBER 10

Noah beseeched Us and We graciously answered his prayers, thus saving him and his
household from a great distress, thereby allowing his descendants to survive. Thus We
granted him the praise of later generations that
shall say, "Peace be on Noah in all humanity."
Thus We reward the good.

THOSE WHO SET THE RANKS 37:75–80

*The pleas of the oppressed, the prayers of eq-
uitable sovereigns, and the worship of the devoted just before they break their fast reach
beyond the doors of heaven and move the
mercy of God.*

The Prophet Muhammad, as reported by
Abu Hurairah, *Al-Hadis,* 3:717

OCTOBER 11

He said, "I seek refuge in my Lord, who will guide me." Then he implored, "My Lord, bless me with righteous offspring." And We gave him the glad tidings of a gentle son. When his son came of age, Abraham said, "My son, I had a dream that I am sacrificing you. I urge you to tell me what you think." He replied, "Do as you are bidden, and by Allah's will you shall find me steadfast." Then both father and son surrendered before the will of Allah. Abraham had laid his son prostrate when We called out to him and said, "Abraham, you have already fulfilled your vision." Thus We reward the good. For that indeed was a test.

THOSE WHO SET RANKS 37:99–106

Abraham said, "Depart out of the way! You [Gabriel] are but an emissary. After the direct vision you are only in the way." Much affliction, agony, and faith are required to deliver the pure from the words of an emissary.

Rumi, *Mathnawi*, 4:2977, 2985

OCTOBER 12

Bear with what they say, and remember Our servant David who was endowed with incredible might and always turned to Us in repentance. Behold, We compelled the mountains to join him in praise of their Lord in the morning and evening, and the birds in all their assemblies were also obedient to him. We made his kingdom strong and endowed him with wisdom and astute judgment.

SAD 38:17–21

God made the oceans subject to man.
Calmly look into their depths.
They are inside yourself.
The four streams of Paradise are ours to direct,
not by our genius but by the command of God.

Rumi, *Mathnawi*, 1:3558, 3560

OCTOBER 13

Thus said the Lord, "Those of you who have transgressed, sinning against your own souls, despair not of your Lord's mercy, for He absolves all sins. Verily He is the Most Forgiving, the Merciful."

THE TROOPS 39:53

Water said to the defiled, "Hurry come to me."

The defiled replied, "But I feel ashamed before the water."

Water said, "But without me how will you wash your shame? How will your filth be removed?"

Shame hinders the faith of the tainted who hide from the water.

Rumi, Mathnawi, 2:1366–68

OCTOBER 14

Allah shall deliver those who warded off evil and remained conscious of Him. No evil shall touch them, nor shall they grieve. Allah creates everything, and He alone is the Guardian of all things.

THE TROOPS 39:61–62

Once Luqman was asked how he had attained such merit. He replied, "By adhering to virtue, by fulfilling all pledges, and by giving up futile apprehensions."

The Prophet Muhammad, as reported by
Malek bin Hawari, *Al-Hadis*, 1:466

OCTOBER 15

Those who remain conscious of their Lord shall be led in multitudes toward Paradise. When they reach it they shall find its doors wide open, and its wardens shall welcome them saying, "Peace be upon you; you have fared well. Enter this Garden of Delight and dwell therein forever." And they shall say: "Praise be to Allah, who fulfilled His promise and made us the inheritors of this land, in which may we dwell as we please. How splendid is the reward of the righteous!"

THE TROOPS 39:73–74

This world is an abode of troubles; the world hereafter of terrors. Humans are in the midst of troubles or terrors until they reach the final abode of Paradise or Hell. Happy is the soul that has detached itself from troubles and terrors and has attached itself to God alone.

Al-Hujwiri, *The Kashf al-Mahjub*, p. 123

OCTOBER 16

Those who bear the throne and all who stand around it hymn the praises of their Lord and implore forgiveness for those who have attained faith saying, "Our Lord! You embrace all things with grace and knowledge. Absolve the sins of those who repent and follow Your way. Save them from the scourge of Hell."

THE BELIEVER 40:7

True repentance entails constant regret of your sins. Without remorse, good deeds, be they abounding, could be eclipsed by pride that follows piety. Remorse for a sin is superior to good works. Never forget your transgressions to save yourself from conceit.

Al-Hujwiri, *The Kashf al-Mahjub*, p. 296

OCTOBER 17

He reveals His portents to you and sends down sustenance for you from the sky. Yet none pay heed save those who turn to Him repentant. Therefore worship your Lord and none other but Him, however much the non-believers be averse.

THE BELIEVER 40:13–14

Turn to Allah and know that Allah will protect you. Seek His help alone, for all the people of this world put together would not be able to benefit you unless Allah wills so.

The Prophet Muhammad, as reported by Abd'Allah ibn Abbas, *Al-Hadis,* 1:445

OCTOBER 18

Moses said, "I seek refuge in my Lord and your Lord from every arrogant person who does not believe in the Day of Reckoning." Then one of the Pharaoh's kinsmen who had kept his true faith a secret said, "Would you kill a man merely because he says, 'My Lord is Allah,' even though he has brought clear evidence to you from his Lord? If he is lying let his lie be upon him, but if he is telling the truth, then some of the scourge that he warns you of may strike you. For Allah does not guide prodigal liars."

THE BELIEVER 40:27–28

There are two kinds of speeches and two kinds of silences. Speech is either truth or a falsification, and silence is either fruition or heedlessness. If one speaks the truth, his words are better than his silence, but he who invents falsifications, his silence is better than his speech.

Al-Hujwiri, *The Kashf al-Mahjub*, p. 356

OCTOBER 19

Then he who was a true believer said, "Follow me, my people, that I may show you the right path. The life of this world is but a momentary comfort, but the life of the hereafter is everlasting. There the transgressors shall be paid with the like thereof, and the righteous, whether male or female, shall enter Paradise where blessings beyond reckoning will be theirs. My people, why is it that I invite you toward salvation, but you entice me to the Fire?"

THE BELIEVER 40:38–41

The divine breath came, saw you, and departed.
It gave life to whom it would and departed.
Another breath has arrived.
Be heedful; do not miss this chance.
It extinguished the fire of the soul on fire
and gave the dead soul vitality of life.

Rumi, *Mathnawi,* 1:1953–55

306

OCTOBER 20

It is Allah who appointed the earth as a dwelling place for you and the sky as a canopy above. He brought you into being and perfected your forms and provided provender to sustain you. Such is Allah, your Lord, blessed be He, the Lord of the worlds, the Eternal! There is no other God save Him. So worship Him alone and none other. Praise be to Allah, the Lord of the worlds!

THE BELIEVER 40:64–65

I said, "Many a tear I shed in separation from you."

He replied, "Why grieve? Every tear will be turned into a precious pearl."

I said, "Many a night I have lain awake."

He replied, "For every such night you shall gain a hundred nights."

Rumi, *The Life and Thought of Rumi*, p. 138

OCTOBER 21

He placed lofty mountains rising high above the earth and bestowed His blessings upon it and in four days provided means of sustenance for all alike. Then He turned to the heavens that were but a cloud of smoke and said to both the heavens and the earth, "Come both of you willingly or unwillingly." They replied, "We come in total submission." Next He ordained the seven heavens into being in two days and assigned to each its own function. The lowest heaven He adorned with brilliant stars and rendered them impregnable. Such is the command of the Almighty, the All-Knowing.

FUSILAT 41:10–12

Lord, if I worship You from the fear of Hell, then let me burn in Hell. If I worship You for the hope of Paradise, then deny me admittance to it. But if I worship You out of reverence for You alone, then do not deny me the joy of Your Eternal Beauty.

Rabiʻa, in *Rabiʻa the Mystic*, p. 30

OCTOBER 22

Those who say, "Our Lord is Allah," and follow the right path, angels descend upon them saying, "Fear not, nor grieve, but rejoice in Paradise, which you have been promised." We are your protecting friends in the life of the world and in the hereafter, and there you shall have all that your souls desire, and all that you prayed for.

FUSILAT 41:30–31

By his noble aim he achieved a high rank, though he confused the imposter with the sheikh. The imposter has a dearth of soul within, but we have a dearth of bread without. Why should we hide our want like the imposter and suffer for the sake of false reputation?

Rumi, *Mathnawi*, 1:2284, 2286–87

OCTOBER 23

Who is better of speech than the one who invites others to the service of the Lord, is upright himself, and proclaims, "I am of those who surrendered themselves to Allah." Good and evil deeds are not alike; offset evil with good, and then he who was your enemy shall become your true friend. Only those who remain patient in adversity achieve such goodness; indeed they are blessed with good fortune. Nonetheless if Satan ever tempts you, seek refuge in Allah. For He hears all and comprehends all.

FUSILAT 41:33–36

If you stay patient when moved to anger and forgive a wrong, Allah will protect you as His close friend; only your foes will be disgraced.

The Prophet Muhammad, as reported by Abd'Allah ibn Abbas, *Al-Hadis*, 1:479

OCTOBER 24

Whoever does good, it is to the advantage of his own soul, and his wickedness shall also be against his own soul. Your Lord is not in the least unjust.

FUSILAT 41:46

Once I went to pay my respects to a great sheikh. My rough garments looked filthy and worn with use. When I found the sheikh, he was seated on a couch clothed in the finest linen. Offended, I thought, "This man claims to be a saint yet surrounds himself with luxury, and look at me! How can he claim to forsake the world? I cannot submit to his teachings."

Reading my thoughts, he replied, "Some reflect on God and are rich in God, and others occupy themselves with self-mortification." Instantly I regretted fostering such pride and implored God's forgiveness.

Abu Sa'id al-Mayhani,
The Kashf al-Mahjub, p. 165

OCTOBER 25

As for those who choose protecting friends beside Him, Allah is well aware of them; you are not responsible for them. Thus We revealed to you the Qur'an in Arabic that you may warn the mother-town [Mecca] and those around it. Forewarn them of the inevitable Day of Congregation, when some will dwell in Paradise and some burn in Hell.

COUNSEL 42:6–7

I never saw anyone as just as the world. As long as you pursue the world it will pursue you, but when you turn away from it and seek God, it will leave you alone and its glamour shall no longer fascinate you.

Al-Hujwiri, *The Kashf al-Mahjub*, p. 147

October 26

It is He who sends down the saving rain after despair and extends His limitless mercy, the Protecting Friend, the Praiseworthy. Among His signs are the creation of the heavens and the earth and all the living creatures that have been dispersed therein. And He has the dominion to gather them before Him when He will. The misfortunes that befall you are the fruits of your own labors, since He is forever forgiving.

COUNSEL 42:28–30

They possess free will and confinement alike. Like raindrops they become pearls inside the oyster shell. Mere raindrops outside the shell, inside they become precious pearls.

Rumi, *The Life and Thought of Rumi*, p. 165

OCTOBER 27

Whatever you are given is but for the enjoyment of life in this world, whereas that which is with God is far better and more enduring. It shall be given to those who stay away from deplorable sins and indecencies and forgive amiably when roused to anger, who establish worship and obey the commandments of their Lord, who manage their affairs by mutual counsel and give in alms of what We have bestowed upon them, nevertheless who also defend themselves when wronged. The recompense of an evil deed is the like evil, but those who forgive and seek atonement, Allah shall duly reward them. For Allah does not hold the wrongdoers dear.

COUNSEL 42:36–40

The Prophet said that God has said,
"I cannot be contained in hallowed places.
Heaven and earth cannot hold Me.
But I am contained by true hearts.
If you seek Me, search in those hearts."

Rumi, *Mathnawi*, 1:2653–55

OCTOBER 28

Hold fast to what has been revealed to you. You are indeed on the right path. This Qur'an most doubtlessly is an exhortation for you and your people; however, all shall be examined for their conduct and the assertion of their faith.

ORNAMENTS OF GOLD 43:43

Prayer is an instrument through which novices find their path to God. Thus ablution symbolizes repentance; the Qibla,[18] a spiritual guide; standing in prayer becomes self-mortification; the recitation of the Qur'an, inner meditation; bowing the head, humility; prostration, self-knowledge; profession of faith, intimacy; and salutation becomes detachment from the world and bondage of stations.

Al-Hujwiri, The Kashf al-Mahjub, p. 301

OCTOBER 29

Jesus came with obvious signs of Allah's sovereignty and said, "I have come to you with divine revelations and to render intelligible some of the things that you disagree upon. Therefore, be observant of the Lord and follow me. For Allah without doubt is my Lord and yours. So worship Him, for that is the straight path."

ORNAMENTS OF GOLD 43:63–64

With the exception of Mary and Jesus, all newborns cry at birth because they feel the touch of Satan.

The Prophet Muhammad, as reported by
Abu Hurairah, *Al-Hadis,* 3:132

OCTOBER 30

We have set you on the right path, so follow the truth and do not follow the desires of those who do not know.

CROUCHING 45:18

To know your own illness is the proper remedy. When you repent you feel humility. That is the time to obey the Prophet's command "Have mercy." Why do you presume to be safe and fortunate? Don't you remember God's solace, "Do not fear"?

Rumi, *Mathnawi*, 2:3037, 3039

OCTOBER 31

We have ordained humankind to show kindness toward their parents, for in pain their mothers carry them and in pain do they give birth. In thirty months they bear and wean; thus when they attain maturity they may pray, "Lord, inspire us that we may be thankful for the blessings You bestowed upon us and our parents. Kindle within us the desire to do what is upright and pleasing to You. Grant us righteous offspring, Lord. Verily, we turn to You in repentance, surrendering ourselves in earnest."

WIND-CURVED SAND-HILLS 46:15

A person once asked the Prophet if he could participate in the holy war. The Prophet asked if his mother was still living. "Yes," he replied. "In that case take care of her because Paradise is beneath her feet."

Reported by Muawiyah bin Ja'hema,
Al-Hadis, 1:187

NOVEMBER

NOVEMBER 1

Behold! We have given you a clear victory that
you may be absolved of the sins of your past
and those yet to follow and that the Lord may
perfect His favor to you and guide you and
assist you with His invincible helping hand. It
is but He who fills the hearts of the believers
with peace and reassurance and adds strength
to their conviction. Allah's are the legions of
the heavens and the earth. He alone is the
Knowing, Wise.

VICTORY 48:1–4

*The Prophet said to Ali, "You may be the
Lion of God,*[19] *but depend not on valor alone.
Learn to blossom under the shade of hope. Rejoice in the Sage who cannot be beguiled from
the way."*

Rumi, *Mathnawi*, 1:2959–61

NOVEMBER 2

We sent you [Muhammad] as a witness and a
herald of glad tidings and to admonish, so that
humankind may believe in Allah and his messenger and honor Him and glorify Him morning and evening. Those who pledge allegiance
to you are really pledging their allegiance to
Allah, for the hand of Allah is above their
hands. Those in breach of their oaths break
them to their own disadvantage, and those who
keep their covenant with Allah shall be blessed
with an immense reward.

VICTORY 48:8–10

I am the orchard; You the rain.
Only I need you twenty times more.
Rejoicing in You a beggar receives victuals
without any means or resistance.
We are the fishes; You the ocean of life.
We live by Your favor, O Exalted of All.

Rumi, *Mathnawi*, 3:1338–39, 1341

NOVEMBER 3

When the hearts of the unbelievers were completely hardened by contempt, contempt stemming from the bigotry of ignorance, Allah bestowed the gift of His peace upon His messenger and upon the believers and filled them with the strength of self-restraint, for they were worthy of it. Allah is Aware of all things.

VICTORY 48:26

When reason reaches its peak and the souls of His lovers feel helpless and disabled, they grow restless and stretch their hands in supplication, seeking comfort for their burning souls. When every manner of search within their power has been consumed, the doorway to Him is opened.

Al-Hujwiri, *The Kashf al-Mahjub*, p. 270

NOVEMBER 4

Muhammad is the messenger of Allah. Those who follow him are merciful to one another but relentless toward the infidels. You can see them bowing and prostrating themselves in worship, seeking Allah's favor and His bounty. Their foreheads are marked by the traces of prostration. Their parable in the Torah and the Gospel is as follows: "They are like the seed that sprouts forth its shoot and is strengthened by Him, and is raised firm upon its stalk, delighting the farmers." Thus Allah strengthens the believers that through them He may enrage the infidels. Allah has promised forgiveness and an immense reward to those who believe and do good works.

VICTORY 48:29

His miracles are countless,
the waves of His bounty tide upon tide.
These and a hundred times as many miracles
allow the light of His face
to shine inside and out.

Rumi, *Mathnawi*, 3:1469, 1474

NOVEMBER 5

The believers among themselves are like brothers. Therefore make peace between your brothers, and observe your duty to Allah that you
may obtain mercy. Believers, let no one mock
the other, for it could very well be that they
are better than yourselves, nor let women mock
other women, neither defaming nor insulting
one another by nicknames. Accusation of de-
pravity after faith has been accepted is a great
evil indeed. Those who do not repent are the
actual transgressors.

THE PRIVATE APARTMENTS 49:10–11

*Do not strut proudly on account of your good
deeds. Do not let pride waylay you. When you
deem yourself holier than others, know that
you have fallen into grave error because in your
pride you believed yourself equal to God.*

Sheikh Abdul Qadir Jillani,
Futhul Ghaib, p. 179

NOVEMBER 6

Believers, keep away from excessive suspicion, for suspicion in some cases is a grave crime. Do not spy, nor backbite one another. Would any one of you like to eat the flesh of a dead brother? You certainly abhor that so abhor the other! Remain conscious of Allah, for Allah verily is the Most Relenting and Merciful.

THE PRIVATE APARTMENTS 49:12–13

When your heart is dark as iron,
steadily polish yourself
that the heart may become a mirror,
a beautiful shine reflecting from within.
Although iron is dark and dismal,
polishing clears the darkness away.

Rumi, *Mathnawi*, 4:2469–71

Verily, We created man and We are aware of all that his soul incites him to because We are closer to him than his jugular vein. The two custodians,[20] one seated on his right and the other on his left, observe him. No sooner does he utter a word than it is recorded by a wary watcher. The agony of death brings with it the truth.

QAF 50:16–19

In the valley, on the mountain, I beheld only God.
In hardship I saw Him by my side.
In ease and well-being I beheld only God.
Like a candle I melted in His flame.
Amid the sparks of the flames,
I beheld only God.

Baba Kuhi of Shiraz,
in *Rabi'a the Mystic*, p. 64

NOVEMBER 8

Those who adhere to faith and their offspring who follow them in conviction shall be united in Paradise. They shall not be denied the reward of their true endeavors; each person shall be held responsible for what he earned. There We shall provide them with all the delectable victuals their hearts desire. Passing around from hand to hand they shall drink of a cup that will cause no idle talk nor any desire to sin.

THE MOUNT 52:21–23

This world is a playground and death the night to which you return empty of purse all worn out. The earnings of faith are love and inner peace. The flesh craves all that is passing away. How long will you covet the vile? Let go.

Rumi, *Mathnawi*, 2:2600–2602

NOVEMBER 9

By the setting star, your comrade [Muhammad] has not gone astray, neither is he deceived, nor following his own desire. This Qur'an is a divine inspiration revealed to him by the mighty one [Gabriel]. Endowed with incredible power he made himself manifest on the uppermost horizon of the sky. Then drawing nearer he came downward until he was only two bowlengths away from him. Thus Allah made His revelations manifest to the chosen servant. His own heart did not belie the vision. Then how can you dispute with him?

THE STAR 53:1–12

Those who do not love the Beloved shall not be able to see Him, for one cannot know and see the sun with a lamp.

Al-Ghazzali, in *Masters of the Path*, p. 32

NOVEMBER 10

Those who restrain themselves from the greatest of sins and wickedness, except the unwilled offenses, shall find the Lord full of mercy. He is fully aware of you, from the time He created you from dust, and when you were hidden in your mothers' wombs. Therefore do not pretend to be pure, for He is completely aware of those who are chaste.

THE STAR 53:32

The pleas of the devoted ascend to heaven,
the smoke of their sincerity ascends to heaven,
and the angels entreat God in earnest:
"O You who answer every prayer,
Your protection is being beseeched.
Your devotee in utter humility pleads.
Hear him, Lord.
He knows only to depend on You."

Rumi, *Mathnawi*, 6:4217–19, 4220

NOVEMBER 11

He turned to his Lord and implored, "Help me, Lord, for I am overcome." Then We opened the gates of heaven with pouring rain and caused the earth to burst forth with gushing springs, and the waters gathered for a predestined purpose.

THE MOON 54:10–12

This world is full of remedies. But you have no remedy until God opens a window for you. You may not be aware of that remedy just now. In the hour of need it will be made clear to you. The Prophet said God made a remedy for every pain.

Rumi, *Mathnawi*, 2:682–84

NOVEMBER 12

All living beings that dwell on the earth are doomed to die. Only your Lord's countenance will abide forever, powerful and glorious. Then which of your Lord's blessings will you deny? All those who dwell in the heavens and on the earth entreat Him for sustenance, and every day He executes universal power. Which then of your Lord's blessings will you deny?

THE BENEFICENT 55:26–30

The children of Adam grow old and gray, yet two things never change: their avarice and their longing for an everlasting life.

The Prophet Muhammad, as reported by
Anas bin Malik, *Al-Hadis*, 1:513

NOVEMBER 13

Praise the name of Your Lord, the Magnificent. I swear by the celestial constellations, a solemn oath if you but knew, that this Qur'an, is a glorious enlightenment, well protected in the form of a Book, that only the pure can touch. It is a revelation from the Lord of the worlds. Would you then look down in contempt on a scripture such as this and make your daily living by rejecting it?

THE EVENT 56:74–81

The miraculous quality of the Qur'an is that one never grows weary of reading or listening to it. The Quresh[21] used to come secretly by night and listen in awe to the Prophet recite. One night Utba bin Rabi'a, an eloquent poet of the time, swooned upon hearing a chapter from the Qur'an. He later swore, "I am positive those are not the words of a mortal."

Al-Hujwiri, *The Kashf al-Mahjub*, p. 394

NOVEMBER 14

When the soul of the dying man takes its last breath and you look on helplessly, We are closer to him than you are, though you cannot see Us. If you feel you do not depend on Us, why do you not restore life, if what you say is indeed the truth? Then if the deceased is righteous, he will find fulfillment in the Garden of Delight.

THE EVENT 56:83–89

*One engrossed in Your thought
is oblivious to the world.
One wounded by Your shaft
is indebted to no servant.
If I suffer even a thousand woes in Your love,
I do not feel the pain when You are with me.*

A Sufi poem, in *Islamic Sufism*, p. 88

NOVEMBER 15

All that is in the heavens and on the earth glorifies Allah. He alone is the Almighty, the Cognizant, the Sovereign of the heavens and the earth, who bestows life and ordains death, and has complete power over all things. He is the First and the Last, the Manifest and the Unseen, the One and the Only with the knowledge of all things.

IRON 57:1–3

God created the hearts of men to be the homes of His praise, but they have become the homes of lust; nothing but fear and a desire for goodness can purify them. When faith establishes itself within the heart, praise and contentment follow.

Abu Muhammad bin Khubayq,
The Kashf al-Mahjub, p. 128

NOVEMBER 16

He bestows a clear revelation upon His slave
that you may be led out of darkness into light.
Indeed Allah is most compassionate and merciful toward you. Why would you not spend
in the way of Allah, when the entire heritage
of the heavens and the earth belongs to Him?
Those of you who spent in the cause of Allah
and fought before the victory [the conquest of
Mecca] will be held in a higher esteem than
those who gave in alms and fought thereafter.
Though Allah promised an abundant generosity
to all, He is cognizant of all you do.

IRON 57:9–10

*God has the power to touch the heart of the
sinner, to turn him away from his wicked ways.*

Rabi'a, in *Rabi'a the Mystic,* p. 57

NOVEMBER 17

On that day you see the believers, both men and women, their light shining before them and on their right hands, they will be told: "Wonderful news for you today: hereon you shall dwell eternally in the Gardens of bliss. Indeed this is a supreme triumph." On that day the hypocrites, both men and women, shall beseech the believers and say, "Look toward us that we may borrow some of your light," but they will be told, "Go back and seek your light over there [on earth]." At that they will be separated by a wall with a gate in it. Then those on the inside shall be blessed with mercy, but those left outside shall suffer the doom of Hell-fire.

Iron 57:12–13

The highest person is he who is of most use to humankind.

'Ali bin Abi Talib,
in Masters of the Path, p. 4

NOVEMBER 18

Beware, the life of this world is nothing but a pastime, a momentary delight. It is but empty bragging, a pursuit of wealth and children. It is like the vegetation that flourishes after rain and is a source of delight to the farmer; but soon it turns yellow and withers away, crumbling into worthless waste. But in the life to come an eternal contentment or a grievous suffering awaits you. The life of this world is only an illusion.

IRON 57:20

When a lover of God turns his eyes away from the temptations of this world, he sees the Lord with the eyes of his heart.

Al-Hujwiri, *The Kashf al-Mahjub*, p. 330

NOVEMBER 19

No disaster, unless it has been preordained and recorded in the book of records, can ever befall the earth nor your own selves. Behold, all this is easy enough for Allah. Know this so that you may not despair for the good fortune you lost, nor exult unduly because of the blessings bestowed upon you. Allah does not love the arrogant and the boastful.

IRON 57:22–23

In separation from God you have become arrogant; pay heed before His scourge strikes you down. Do not exult because of your good fortune. Over and again God admonishes you with the examples of the transgressors before you. If you really want to enjoy the limitless bounty of Allah, surrender yourselves before His will and endure all afflictions with fortitude.

Sheikh Abdul Qadir Jillani,
Fayuz E Yazdani, p. 30

NOVEMBER 20

Are you not aware that Allah is cognizant of all that is in the heavens and on the earth? Therefore, if three consult in secret He is the fourth; if five, He is the sixth. Whether they be fewer or more, He is always with them, wherever they may be. And then He will inform them on the Day of Resurrection of all their deeds. Behold, Allah is aware of all things. Therefore, believers, whenever you hold secret conferences, do not conspire together for wickedness and disobedience and enmity toward the messenger. Inspire each other toward piety, and remain devoted to Allah, before whom you shall all be gathered.

SHE THAT DISPUTED 58:7, 9

The devil reposes in the hearts of all human beings. When they are mindful of Allah he retracts; but when they are heedless, he whispers evil in their thoughts.

The Prophet Muhammad, as reported by
Abu Hurairah, *Al-Hadis,* 3:732

November 21

Believers, when you are told to make room in assemblies, make room; in return Allah will make room for you in the hereafter. And when you are told to rise [for a good deed], rise up. Allah will exalt those who are truly faithful and have been endowed with knowledge, for Allah is observant of all that you do.

SHE THAT DISPUTED 58:11

Almighty Allah said, "Search for Me among the weak, for verily through them shall you be given provision."

The Prophet Muhammad, as reported by Abu Darda'a, *Al-Hadis,* 1:269

NOVEMBER 22

And that wealth [the booty of war] is for the poor refugees who have been forced to flee their homes, forsaking everything, seeking sustenance only from Allah. That wealth is also for those who help Allah and His messenger and for those who remained in their city and embraced the faith before them and welcomed those who came to them seeking refuge, who do not begrudge them for what they have been given, but value them above themselves, though they may be impoverished themselves.[22] Those who are able to save themselves from avarice shall certainly prevail.

EXILE 59:8–9

The best charity is to satisfy a hungry person.

The Prophet Muhammad, as reported by
Anas bin Malik, *Al-Hadis,* 1:280

NOVEMBER 23

Believers, why do you say what you do not execute? It is most offensive in the sight of Allah when you say what you do not practice!

THE RANKS 61:2–3

Two basic characteristics can never be found in hypocrites: good conduct and true knowledge of religion.

The Prophet Muhammad, as reported by Abu Hurairah, *Al-Hadis,* 1:437

NOVEMBER 24

Remember when Jesus the son of Mary said, "Children of Israel, behold, I have been sent by Allah as His messenger to confirm what was revealed before me in the Torah, and to bring you the auspicious news of another messenger to follow, whose name shall be Ahmad."[23] Yet when he went before them with evident signs of truth, they said, "This is nothing but sorcery."

THE RANKS 61:6–7

A person with knowledge of God strives to fulfil His commandments and follows the conduct of the Prophet. The nearer one is to God, the more eager he is to do His bidding, and the further he is from God, the more averse he is to follow His Apostle.

Al-Hujwiri, *The Kashf al-Mahjub*, p. 140

NOVEMBER 25

Have faith in Allah and His messenger, and strive in His way with your wealth and your lives. That is for your own good, for He will forgive you for your transgressions and admit you into graceful mansions in the Gardens of bliss where rivers run through. That indeed is the greatest triumph. Deliver the glad tidings to the believers that Allah will bestow yet another blessing upon them, His succor and a speedy victory.

THE RANKS 61:11–13

The divine bounty filled him with peace and strength, strength that helped him cheerfully endure all the afflictions that knocked him about.

Rumi, *Mathnawi*, 3:2341, 2343

NOVEMBER 26

Believers, when you hear the call of prayer
on the day of congregation, hasten to the remembrance of Allah, and cease your worldly
commerce. That is better for you if you but
knew. When the prayer has ended, you may
continue to seek of His bounty; and remain
mindful of Allah that you may gain prosperity.

THE CONGREGATION 62:9–10

*I never hear the call of prayer without re-
membering the trumpet blare on the Day of
Resurrection. I never see the snow without remembering the fluttering scrolls of deeds being
handed out. I never see a swarm of locusts
without remembering the assembly on the Day
of Judgment.*

Rabi'a, in *Rabi'a the Mystic*, p. 142

NOVEMBER 27

No adversity ever occurs except by Allah's will. Then those who remain steadfast shall be guided by Allah onto the right path. Allah is cognizant of all things; obey Him and His messenger. Then should you turn away, bear in mind the duty of Our messenger was only to deliver the message with clarity.

MUTUAL DISILLUSION 64:11–12

Liberated from suffering and search
I have tied myself to the skirt of God.
If I fly, I look at the summits I ascend.
If I go around in circles,
I observe the axis on which I revolve.
If I am dragged by a burden,
I know where I go.
For I am the moon, and the sun is my guide.

Rumi, *Mathnawi*, 1:3807–9

NOVEMBER 28

Whoever remains observant of Allah shall find Allah creating for him a way out from every difficulty and providing for him from sources unimaginable. Anyone who depends on Allah shall find the Lord to be sufficient for him; for Allah's decrees decidedly come to pass. Allah has set a measure for all things.

DIVORCE 65:3

He does not refuse sustenance to the one who speaks ill of Him. How then could He refuse sustenance to the one whose soul is overflowing with love for Him?

Rabi'a, in *Rabi'a the Mystic,* p. 24

NOVEMBER 29

You who believe turn to Allah in repentance,
that your Lord may absolve you of your evil
deeds and admit you into Gardens of Delight.
That day Allah will not debase the Prophet
and his followers. Their light will shine before
them and on their right sides, and they will say,
"Lord, forgive us and perfect our light for us.
Without doubt You alone have the power to
decree all things."

BANNING 66:8

You may have wealth, O mighty monarch,
but it is other than you; one day it will be gone.
Become your own fortune, O chosen one,
before you are left destitute.
Seek the bounty within yourself;
when you are the bounty,
how can you lose yourself?

Rumi, *Mathnawi*, 4:1109–11

NOVEMBER 30

Have they not seen the birds that soar above
them, spreading and constricting their wings in
flight? None save the Beneficent upholds them,
for He watches over everything. Is there any
other who could protect you like armor save
the Beneficent? The unbelievers indeed suffer
from grave self-deception. Should He withhold
your sustenance, is there any other who can
provide for you? Still you persist in your pride
and defiance.

THE SOVEREIGNTY 67:19–21

*Knowledge is the spirit that saves the heart
from the death of ignorance; it is the light
that saves it from the darkness of iniquity.
The hearts of the iniquitous are dead because
they are oblivious to God, and the hearts of
the heedless are sick because they ignore His
commandments.*

Abu Ali Thaqafi,
The Kashf al-Mahjub, p. 17

December

DECEMBER 1

Wait patiently for your Lord's ordinance, and do not be like him [Jonah] who cried out in despair when he was swallowed by the great fish. Had the Lord not bestowed His blessings upon him, he certainly would have been cast on the barren shores in utter disgrace. But his Lord exalted him once more and placed him among the righteous.

THE PEN 68:48–50

If you desire light, be ready to receive light. Nurture vainglory and become separated from light. If you long for a way out of this prison, bow down in worship and draw near.

Rumi, *Mathnawi*, 1:3606–7

December 2

Man certainly was created impulsive, overcome by despondence in misfortune and niggardly when blessed with good fortune. But not so for those who remain constant in worship and set aside a certain portion of their wealth for the beggar and the destitute and believe in the Day of Resurrection and dread their Lord's scourge.

THE ASCENDING STAIRWAYS 70:19–27

Since man is made of clay, he can never be completely pure. Since clay is basically foul, how can humans escape their basic nature? Purity does not lie in rituals, nor can human nature be changed by effort. Those who love God and remain conscious only of their Beloved attain purity.

Al-Hujwiri, *The Kashf al-Mahjub*, p. 32

DECEMBER 3

Why do you deny the Majesty of Allah, who created you in stages? Do you not see the seven heavens, one above the other in complete harmony, the bright sun and the reflecting moon? He created you from dust, and to dust shall you return. Then once again He will resurrect you.

NOAH 71:13–18

The light of love and union with God is like the light of the sun and the moon shining together. The light of the sun and moon is worthless before the light of love. Visual perception can only see the sun and the moon or the skies, but the eye of the heart witnesses the empyrean.

Al-Hujwiri, *The Kashf al-Mahjub,* p. 33

DECEMBER 4

Some among us are righteous and others corrupt. We have many sects that follow different paths. We now know that we cannot escape Allah, neither on the earth nor in flight. We heard the Book of Guidance and we believed therein. Those who believe in the Lord should fear neither privation nor oppression.

THE JINN 72:11–14

When Shibli heard the verse "And remember your Lord when you forget," he declared, "The need for remembrance arises because of forgetfulness. The world has stopped remembering Him." At that a loud shriek escaped his lips, and he fainted. Upon regaining consciousness, he said, "The universe is lost in His praise, except the humans. I wonder at those who hear the dictates of God, yet continue to transgress."

Shibli, *The Kashf al-Mahjub,* p. 395

DECEMBER 5

Only Allah holds the knowledge of the unseen and does not reveal these mysteries to anyone, except those He selects as His messengers. He watches over them through guardians that advance before and shield them from behind that He may observe the proper delivery of His message. He is aware of all that they do and maintains a strict record of all things that exist.

THE JINN 72:26–28

When Nimrod condemned Abraham to a pit of fire, Gabriel visited him and asked, "Is there anything that I can do for you?"

Abraham answered, "I stand in desperate need, but I shall not ask you."

"Then ask God," replied Gabriel.

"My Lord is aware of my plight, and only He knows why I must endure this; therefore I need not ask." And the fire turned cold.

Al-Hujwiri, *The Kashf al-Mahjub*, p. 73

DECEMBER 6

Without doubt the impressions of the mind are the strongest and the speech most articulate in the vigil at night. During the day you are engaged by the activities of life. So remember the name of your Lord, and devote yourself to Him with all your heart. He is the Lord of the East and the West, and there is no other deity besides Him. Elect Him alone to protect you, and patiently bear what they say, and avoid their company without any disagreement.

THE ENSHROUDED ONE 73:6–10

When God fills an adept with the desire to comprehend His essence, knowledge becomes vision, vision revelation, revelation contemplation, and contemplation existence in God. Words are hushed to silence, life becomes death, explanations come to an end, signs are effaced, and disputes are cleared up.

Junayd, in *Rabi'a the Mystic*, p. 95

December 7

Behold, your Lord is aware of how you strive for Him, staying awake at nights, sometimes two-thirds, sometimes half, and at others a third thereof, as do some of your followers. Allah alone determines the length of the night and the day and is aware that you will not be able to continue the vigil. Thus He turned to you in mercy. Recite then as much of the Qur'an as you can with ease, because He knows that some among you are sick, others must travel in search of His bounty, and others still have to struggle in His cause. Recite then only that which is easy for you, establish worship and give in alms, thus offering Allah a generous loan. Whatever good you send before yourselves, you shall find a richer reward with Allah. So seek His forgiveness, for He is the Most Forgiving, the Most Merciful.

THE ENSHROUDED ONE 73:20

Hundreds of thousands of inner eyes were opened and through Your breath made ready to reflect upon the unseen.

Rumi, *Mathnawi*, 3:2500

358

DECEMBER 8

O you wrapped in a cloak,[24] arise and warn!
Magnify your Lord and purify your raiment,
and stay away from defilement. Do not grant
favors expecting worldly gains in return; instead turn to your Lord and remain patient.

THE CLOAKED ONE 74:1–7

My peace, my brothers, is in solitude,
because my beloved is with me.
His love is my test among the mortal beings....
Zeal for His union has healed my soul.

Rabi'a, in *Rabi'a the Mystic*, p. 12

DECEMBER 9

The righteous shall drink of a cup mixed with the elixir of Kafur, a gushing spring made for the chosen that keep their vows and fear the torments of the Day of Judgment, those who though in dire need themselves sustain the orphans, feed the wretched and the enslaved, and say, "We sustain you for the sake of Allah and expect no reward nor gratitude from you in return."

Time or Man 76:5–9

Seek what you wish from God, not from men.
Be satisfied in joy; there is honor therein.
On friends and relatives be not a burden.
Rich is he who hopes from God, not from men.

Al-Ghazzali, *Ihya Ulum Id-Din*, 4:175

DECEMBER 10

We revealed the Qur'an over a gradual period of time.[25] (In the same manner) wait in patience as commanded by your Lord, and do not yield to the ways of the ungracious or the wicked. Remember your Lord in the morning and the evening, worshiping and prostrating yourselves before Him through the vigil of the night. Behold the unbelievers who love this fleeting life and remain forgetful of the Day of Anguish!

TIME OR MAN 76:23–27

Abu Bakr al-Saddiq once said, "This world is transitory and our life therein but a moment borrowed, our breaths numbered, yet our indifference reckless."

Al-Hujwiri, *The Kashf al-Mahjub*, p. 70

DECEMBER 11

Have We not spread the earth like a resting place and the made mountains its supports? Indeed We did, as We created you in pairs, and made sleep for you to repose. And We made the night as a blanket, and the day for subsistence. We created above you seven impregnable heavens and positioned the sun as a brilliant lamp.

THE TIDINGS 78:6–13

Being observant of God is an act of devotion toward God. Sleep is an act of God drawing us near. That which is conferred upon us by God without our choice is positively superior to that which we send to Him. Sleep therefore is a wonderful gift of God bestowed upon His creatures.

Junayd, *The Kashf al-Mahjub*, p. 352

DECEMBER 12

There [in Heaven] they shall hear no vain discourse, nor any prevarication. All this will be a splendid reward from your Lord, the Sovereign of the heavens and the earth and all that lies in between, the Beneficent with whom no one shall have the power to converse. On the day when the angels and the Spirit stand according to their ranks, they shall not be able to utter a word, save those who receive consent of the Merciful and declare what is right.

THE TIDINGS 78:35–38

Strive for Paradise. A small nook within its bliss is better than the whole world and all the riches within.

The Prophet Muhammad, as reported by
Abu Hurairah, *Al-Hadis,* 4:162

DECEMBER 13

Those who stand in awe before the Lord and constrain their souls from transgressing shall find their abode in Paradise. They ask you when the hour of doom shall strike. But how can you tell them? Only your Lord holds that knowledge. Your mission is only to warn those who fear it.

THOSE WHO DRAG FORTH 79:40–45

I surrender myself to no other god but God.
If He desires my bloodshed,
then so be it! I have no fear.
I may be disgraced in your world;
before God honor will be mine.
A laughing stock in the eyes of the world,
in God's eyes cherished and acclaimed.

Rumi, *Mathnawi*, 3:1076–78

DECEMBER 14

He [Muhammad] frowned and turned away because a blind man came to him.[26] How could you tell, he may have grown in piety, or taken heed and profited from Our counsel? But you paid attention to the arrogant wealthy who deem themselves self-sufficient.

HE FROWNED 80:1–5

God asked, "What did you earn in your term of respite?" When he heard these words in his prayer, from shame he bent downward in complete awe. From shame he could stand no more; with knees bent he prostrated himself and glorified God.

Rumi, *Mathnawi*, 3:2149, 2155–56

DECEMBER 15

When all the souls are reunited with their bodies and the young girl buried alive is asked for what grievous sin she was slain,[27] when the scrolls of deeds will be laid open and the sky torn asunder, the Hell Fire ignited and Paradise brought closer in view: then all souls shall know what they earned in the world.

THE OVERTHROWING 81:7–14

What did you accomplish in your life? How did you consume your sustenance and strength? Where did you lose the luster of your eyes? Where did you lose all the five senses? I gave you bounty. Where is your gratitude? I gave you the capital. Come show me the interest.

Rumi, *Mathnawi*, 3:2150–51, 2164–65

DECEMBER 16

O people! What evil temptation lured you away
from your Lord, who created you, propor-
tioned you, and endowed you with an upright
form? He molded you into whatever form He
willed; yet you deny the Day of Judgment. Behold, there are watchers guarding over you,
noble guardians, who record all that you say
and are aware of all that you do. Verily the
righteous shall dwell in delight, and the wicked
burn in Hell.

THE CLEAVING 82:6–14

*Once a powerful man of Basra detected the
beautiful wife of the gardener as he strolled in
the courtyard. Overcome by lust, he sent the
gardener on an errand and ordered his wife to
lock all the gates.*

*"I already have," she replied, "but one gate
I cannot."*

"And which one is that?" he asked furiously.

*"The gate which lies between the two of us
and Allah." Shaken by the answer, the man
instantly pleaded with God for mercy.*

Al-Hujwiri, *The Kashf al-Mahjub*, p. 13

DECEMBER 17

Behold the wicked who used to mock the believers, and gestured one another in contempt
as they passed them by, and ridiculed them as
they returned home, and claimed when they
saw them, "Look at those who have gone
astray." Yet they were never sent as their guardians. So on that day the righteous will slight
the unbelievers as they recline on their couches
looking around (in wonder).

DEFRAUDING 83:29–35

*Those loved by God are held in contempt by
the vulgar, and those who deem themselves virtuous may not be so in the eyes of God....
Public ridicule is the very sustenance of the chosen of God. They rejoice in it, just as others
rejoice in popularity, for they know that it is
a sign that they are close to Him. As God
said, "My chosen are hidden under My cloak.
Besides Me, only the elect know who they are."*

Al-Hujwiri, *The Kashf al-Mahjub*, p. 63

DECEMBER 18

We shall enlighten you with our revelations in a manner that you will not forget, save that which Allah may will. Behold, We are aware of all that is hidden and that which is manifest, and We will guide you to the easiest path. Therefore admonish others whether this admonition avails or not. Those who fear the Lord will pay heed.

THE MOST HIGH 87:7–10

Once Ibrahim bin Adham saw a stone with the inscription, "Turn me over and read!" When he did an inscription appeared: "You do not practice what you know. Why do you seek what you do not know?"

Al-Hujwiri, *The Kashf al-Mahjub*, p .12

DECEMBER 19

Did We not endow them with two eyes, a tongue, and two lips, and show them the two ways (of good and evil)? Still they did not attempt the ascent. If only they understood what the ascent is. It is to free a captive, to feed an orphan or a near of kin or some miserable wretch in the days of famine, and to remain virtuous, urging others toward compassion and fortitude.

THE CITY 90:8–17

I was given the choice between wisdom and prophecy. I chose wisdom because I could not stand the burden.

Luqman, in *Islamic Sufism*, p. 332

DECEMBER 20

Your Lord has not forsaken you, nor is He averse to you. Behold, the life to come will be far better than the present. Your Lord will bless you and fill you with serenity. Did He not protect you when you were orphaned? And guide you when you were in error? Enrich you when you were in want? Therefore, never wrong the orphan, nor reproach the beggar, but always glorify the blessing of your Lord.

THE MORNING HOURS 93:3–11

"Help your brother whether he is the oppressor or the oppressed." At that a person asked, *"I can help the oppressed, but how can I help the oppressor?"* *"By preventing him from wrongdoing,"* replied the Prophet.

Reported by Anas bin Malik,
Al-Hadis, 1:292

DECEMBER 21

Did We not comfort your heart and relieve you of the burden weighing down your back? Did We not exalt your renown? Every hardship is followed by comfort. Indeed every hardship is followed by comfort.

SOLACE 94:1–6

You are the sole companion of my heart, though my body is available for those who wish its company. This body is hospitable to its guests; the love of my heart is the guest of my soul.

Rabiʻa, in *Rabiʻa the Mystic*, p. 98

DECEMBER 22

Read, in the name of your Lord who created, created man from a clot of blood. Read, for your Lord is the Most Bountiful, the One who taught by the pen, taught man what he did not know.

THE CLOT 96:1–5

When the craft of making armor was made known, iron became wax in your hands. The mountains became your accompanists; they chant the psalms along with you, like those who teach the recitation of the Qur'an with you.

Rumi, *Mathnawi*, 3:2498–99

DECEMBER 23

Behold, We revealed the Qur'an on the Night of Power.[28] If only you knew what the Night of Power is. That one night surpasses a thousand months, for the angels and the Spirit [Gabriel] descend to the earth, bearing divine inspiration by the permission of their Lord. That night is the night of peace until the crack of dawn.

POWER 97:1–5

I once asked the Prophet to tell me what to ask for if I were to identify the Night of Power. He replied, "Say, Lord! You who are the Most Compassionate, the Most Relenting, forgive me for my transgressions."

Reported by A'ishah bint Abi Bakr,
Al-Hadis, 3:555

DECEMBER 24

By the declining day, humankind is at a great disadvantage, save those who do good works, admonish one another to be forthright, and inspire each other to endure hardship.

THE DECLINING DAY 103:1–3

Lord, the night is gone. The dawn has lighted the sky. How I long to know if You accepted or rejected my prayers. Comfort me, Lord, for only you can comfort this state of mine. You gave me life and nurtured me; Yours is all the praise. If You would ever drive me away from Your door, I would never abandon it for the sake of Your love, which I carry in my heart.

Rabi'a, in *Rabi'a the Mystic*, p. 27

DECEMBER 25

Enjoin upon them worship of the Lord of the House,[29] who sustained them in the days of hunger and secured them against fear.

QURESH 106:1–4

As God has made the Qibla[30] manifest, abandon your search. Hark, turn away from all futile search, now that the House has come to view. If you forget this Qibla for one moment, you will be overcome by the qibla of desires.

Rumi, *Mathnawi*, 6:2626–28

December 26

Behold, We bestowed abundance upon you. Therefore worship your Lord and sacrifice for Him. It is your enemy who will be severed from all good.

Abundance 108:1–3

Very high, very grand, and very wide is the ocean of God, the Water of Life. You went after the form and were lead astray. How can you see it? You abandoned the truth. Sometimes it is named "tree," sometimes "sun," sometimes "ocean," sometimes "cloud," one thing from which scores of discoveries arise, its slightest definition an everlasting life.

Rumi, *Mathnawi*, 2:3669–72

December 27

Say, "You who disbelieve, I do not worship that which you venerate, nor do you worship whom I adore. I shall never invoke those whom you invoke, nor will you obey whom I revere. You have your religion, and I have mine."

THE UNBELIEVERS 109:1–6

O You who seek God, know this:
We are the mirrors of God, the absolute Truth.
Come into this tavern of ruin, O clever one;
drink of this cup and see our purity.

Nur Ali Shah, in *Masters of the Path,* p. 94

DECEMBER 28

When Allah's help and victory come and you witness humankind embracing the religion of Allah in throngs, then celebrate the praises of your Lord and implore His forgiveness. Indeed He is the Most Forgiving.

HELP 110:1–3

You see throngs of afflicted feeble folk seated at the door in ardent hope. O you who are crushed, your pleas have been heard. Hark! Rush toward the mercy of God and be delivered of pain. How often has your disease been cured? How often has your soul been delivered of grief?

Rumi, *Mathnawi*, 3:302–4, 308

DECEMBER 29

Say, "He is Allah, the One and Only, the Eternal, beseeched by all. He begot not, nor was He begotten. None can ever be compared to Him."

THE SINCERITY 112:1–4

A group of Hebrew scholars once came to the Prophet and said, "The Lord our God created the angels from light, man from clay, Satan from fire, the heavens from smoke, and the earth from foam. Now tell us about your Lord. What is He made of?" There was a momentary pause before Gabriel inspired Muhammad with the verses of Sincerity.

Cited in *Tehfim ul Qur'an*, p. 531

DECEMBER 30

Say: "I seek refuge in the Lord of Daybreak from the evils of created things, from the doom of the darkness when it is intense, from the hexes of the conjuring witches, and from the malevolence of the envious when he envies."

THE DAYBREAK 113:1–5

When a magician sleeps, so does his sorcery and his craft. When the shepherd sleeps, the wolf becomes assertive. But he who has made God his shepherd, how can the wolf make him prey? The alchemy of God is trustworthy and true. It is villainous to confuse it with sorcery.

Rumi, *Mathnawi*, 3:1192–95

DECEMBER 31

Say, "I seek refuge in the Lord of humankind, the Sovereign of humankind, the God of
humankind, from the evils of the sneaking In-
citer who whispers, whispers in the hearts of
humankind, be it about the jinn [spirits] or
humankind."

HUMANKIND 114:1–6

O Merciful, transform my fears into hope. In
the name of Your glorious Qur'an relent to-
ward me. Allow its light to illumine my way;
endow me with the resolve to follow its dic-
tates. Help me recite it night and day that its
wisdom might blossom within my soul.

A prayer upon finishing the Qur'an

BIBLIOGRAPHY

Translations of the Qur'an

Holy Quran. English trans. Marmaduke Pickthall; Urdu trans. Maulana Fateh Mohammed Jallendhri. Lahore, Pakistan: Taj Company, n.d.

The Message of the Qur'an. English trans. Muhammad Asad. Gibraltar: Dar al-Andalus, 1980.

The Koran with a Parallel Arabic Text. English trans. N. J. Dawood. London and New York: Penguin Books, 1995.

Roman Transliteration of the Holy Qur'an, with Full Arabic Text. English trans. Abdullah Yusuf Ali. 3d ed. Lahore, Pakistan, Sh. Muhammad Ashraf, 1938.

The Holy Qur'an. Urdu trans. Maulana Maududi. Lahore, Pakistan: Idara e Tarjumane Al-Qur'an, n.d.

Holy Qur'an. English trans. M. H. Shakir. Elmhurst, N.Y.: Tehrike Tarssile Qur'an, Inc., n.d.

Other Works

Al-Hadis: An English Translation and Commentary of Miskat-ul-Masabih (Containing Sayings, Doings and Teachings of the Holy Prophet and Events before and after Resurrection). Ed. and trans. Al-Haj Maulana Fazlul Karim. 3d ed. 4 vols. New Delhi: Islamic Book Service, 1994.

Al-Hizbul-A'zam: The Great Prayer Book of Islam. Trans. Ali bin Sultan M. Qari. New Delhi, India: Idara Ishaat-e-Diniyat, n.d.

Fayuz E Yazdani (in Urdu). By Sheikh Abdul Qadir Jillani. Urdu translation by Maulana Aashiq e Ilahi Mairathi. Delhi: Rabani Book Depot, n.d.

Futhul Ghaib (in Urdu). By Sheikh Abdul Qadir Jillani. New Delhi, India: Idara-e-Islamiat, n.d.

Ihya Ulum Id-Din. By Al-Ghazzali. Ed. and trans. Al-Haj Maulana Fazlul-Karim. Book 4. New Delhi, India: Islamic Book Services, 1991.

Islamic Sufism. By Capt. W. B. S. Rabbani. Lahore, Pakistan: Bazam-e-Ittehad-ul-Muslimeen, 1990.

The Kashf al-Mahjub: The Oldest Persian Treatise on Sufism. By 'Ali b. Uthman al-Jullabbi Al-Hujwiri. Trans. Reynold A. Nicholson. Lahore: Sang-e-Meel Publications, 1996. See also the Urdu translation by Maulana Wajid Baksh Sayal published by Feroz Sons Ltd., Lahore.

The Life and Thought of Rumi. By Afzal Iqbal. Lahore, Pakistan: Bazm-i-Iqbal, n.d.

Masters of the Path: A History of the Masters of the Nimatullahi Sufi Order. By Javad Nurbakhsh. London and New York: Khaniqahi-Nimatullahi Publications, 1980.

The Mathnawi of Jallalu'ddin Rumi. Ed. and trans. Reynold A. Nicholson. 6 vols in 3. Lahore: Islamic Book Service, 1989.

Munajat E Maqbool. A Treasury of Supplications. Author unknown. Lahore, Pakistan: Taj Company, n.d.

Rabi'a the Mystic and Her Fellow-Saints in Islam: Being the Life and Teachings of Rabi'a al-'Adawiyya Al-Qaysiyya of Basra Together with Some Account of the Place of the Women Saints in Islam. By Margaret Smith. Lahore, Pakistan: Kazi Publications, 1928.

Sahih al-Bukhari, Summarized. In Arabic and English. Compiled by Al-Imam Zain-ud-Din Ahmad bin Abdul-Lateef Al-Zubaidi. Trans. Muhammad Muhsin Khan. Pahari Bhojla, Delhi, India: Darul Ahya Us-Sunnah, Al Nabawiya, 1994.

Tehfim ul Qur'an (in Urdu). By Abul al Maududi. Urdu translation by Maulana Maududi. Lahore, Pakistan: Idara e Tarjumane Al-Qur'an, n.d.

THE COMPANIONS
OF THE PROPHET AND
THE SUFI MASTERS

The following names are listed in alphabetical order as the names appear in the text. In alphabetizing personal names in Arabic, other conventions are often used, e.g., the article "al-" is ignored. For the benefit of readers not familiar with Arabic names, a simple letter-by-letter sequence is followed here.

Abd'Allah bin Amr. One of Muhammad's most learned companions, he embraced Islam in his sixteenth year.

Abd'Allah bin Mas'ud. The fourth person to convert to Islam.

Abd'Allah bin Mubarak al-Marwazi. 736–97 A.D. Imam of the city of Merv (probably in Iran) renowned for his asceticism and mystic station.

Abd'Allah ibn Abbas. A great orator, one of the closest companions and cousin of the Prophet.

Abd al-Wahid bin Zaid. An eighth-century A.D. ascetic who sanctified worship in solitude.

Abu Ali Thaqafi. An exalted Sufi of the tenth century A.D.

Abu Bakr al-Saddiq. First caliph of the Islamic commonwealth after the death of the Prophet. The closest companion of the Prophet.

Abu Darda'a. A very scholarly Ansar (one of the local residents of Medina who supported the Meccan refugees) who later settled in Syria.

Abu Dharr al-Ghifari. Belonged to the tribe of Ghiffar, a tribe of highway robbers. He became a close companion of the Prophet and converted many of his tribesmen to Islam.

Abu Hurairah, 'Abd al-Rahman al-Dawsi. Arrived in Medina during the campaign of Khayber and being destitute joined "the people of the bench," so called because a long colonnade of the mosque had been set aside for the newcomers who had nowhere to live and had no means of sustenance.

Abu'l-Fayd al-Misri (Abu'l-Fayd Dhu'l-Nun bin Ibrahim al-Misri). A Nubian saint of the ninth century A.D. who suffered persecution all his life. It was not until after his death that his true station was revealed. He was one of the first to develop the theory of annihilation of the self to achieve eternal life.

Abu'l-Hasan (Abu'l-Hasan Muhammad bin Ismael Khayr al-Nassaj). A great sheikh of the eleventh century A.D. who initiated masters like Shibli and Junayd.

Abu'l-Sari Mansur bin Ammar. Though he was from Iraq, he was revered in Iran and had a large following. An ascetic who had full command of the doctrines of religion and mysticism. Ninth century A.D.

Abu Muhammad bin Khubayq. An austere ascetic of the tenth century A.D. who followed the path of poverty.

Abu Sa'id (Abu Sa'id bin Abi al-Khayr). A great Sufi sheikh (spiritual guide) of the eleventh century A.D. Iran. Believed that ritual was necessary only until the soul had been cleansed of carnal desires and had attained union with the Divine.

Abu Sa'id al-Mayhani. An eminent Sufi of the thirteenth century A.D. Well-versed in both science and religion, he had the uncanny ability of reading others' thoughts.

Abu Sayeed al-Khodri. An extremely devout companion who narrated a large number of traditions.

Abu Umamah. A resident of Medina who belonged to the tribe of Aus. He was two years old at the time of the Prophet's death.

A'ishah bint Abi Bakr. The youngest daughter of Abu Bakr al-Saddiq and the wife of the Prophet.

Al-Bar'a bin A'zib. An inhabitant of Kufa, he participated in many campaigns with the Prophet's cousin 'Ali bin Abi Talib. He later settled in Kufa.

Al-Ghazzali, Abu Hameed. A successful professor in Baghdad at the end of the eleventh century A.D. A philosopher who began with reading Sufi books, but found that these teachings cannot be learned through intellectual study.

Al-Hallaj, Hussain Ibn Mansur. The most famous Sufi master of the ninth and the tenth centuries A.D. He spoke the famous words "I am the Truth" and was consequently executed.

Al-Hujwiri, ʻAli bin ʻUthman. Little is known of his life except through his work *Kashf al-Mahjub*. A native of Ghazna, Afghanistan, widely traveled, he received his instruction from many Sufi masters. He died either in A.D. 1063–64 or 1071–72 in Lahore in modern-day Pakistan.

ʻAli bin Abi Talib. The youngest son of the Prophet's uncle Abu Talib. Brought up by the Prophet as his own child and later married his youngest daughter, Fatima. Famous for his valor, he became the fourth caliph of the Islamic commonwealth.

Al-Nuri (Abu'l-Hasan Ahmad bin Muhammad al-Nuri). An austere ascetic weary of flattery. To this day a large number of Sufis follow his teachings.

Al-Razi (Abu Zakariyya Yahya bin Muadh al-Razi). A great sage who held fear and hope to be the wings of salvation.

Al-Sarraj (Abu Nasar al-Sarraj). An eminent Sufi of the tenth century A.D. He justified Sufi thinking as in accordance with the Qur'an.

Al-Zubayr bin al-Awwam. A maternal cousin of the Prophet who embraced Islam at the age of sixteen. Participated in all the campaigns. Martyred and buried in the city of Basra (Iraq).

Anas bin Malik. A faithful servant of the Prophet.

Asma bint Abu Bakr al-Saddiq. The older daughter of Abu Bakr al-Saddiq, the closest friend of the Prophet.

Baba Kuhi of Shiraz. An eminent Sufi of eleventh-century A.D. Iran.

Hasan bin 'Ali. Son of 'Ali bin Abi Talib, grandson of the Prophet. The father of Sufism.

Hatim al-Asamm (Abu 'Abd al-Rahman Hatim bin 'Ulwan al-Asamm). A great Sufi master of Khrusan Iran. He was called the truthful, for it is said he never once lied.

Ibn 'Arabi. An eminent Sufi of the twelfth century A.D., he replaced the idea of a personal God with the concept of Oneness. Only God exists; God is the essence, the substance of everything.

Ibn Umar. The son of Umar bin al-Khattab, the second caliph of the Islamic commonwealth.

'Imran bin Hussain. One of the very close companions of the Prophet, he embraced Islam after the campaign of Khayber. He settled at Basra, where he taught theology.

Ja'bir bin Abd'Allah. A close companion of the Prophet who participated in all the campaigns.

Junayd (Abu'l Qasim al-Junayd). A mystic master of the ninth century A.D. A native of Baghdad and an advocate of love of God as the true path.

Jundub bin Abd'Allah. A descendant of the renowned companion Abu Abd'Allah Ansari. He took part in all the campaigns except the first. He settled in Syria.

Malek bin Hawari. Spent only twenty days in the company of the Prophet. Later he settled in Basra, where he was buried in 716 A.D..

Muawiyah bin Ja'hema. A scribe who later became the governor of Kufa. A companion of the Prophet.

Nayeem bin Mas'ud. One of the refugees who migrated to Medina with the Prophet and participated in the Battle of the Trench.

Nu'man bin Bashir. The governor of Basra, he was eight months old when the Prophet died. He was murdered in 716 A.D..

Nur Ali Shah. A Sufi master of the eighteenth century A.D. A native of Iran.

Rabi'a al-'Adawiyya. A.D. 717–801. An ascetic who followed the path of poverty and self-denial. A mystic famous for her love for God.

Rumi (Jalal al-Din al-Rumi). One of the greatest mystic poets of Persia. Thirteenth century A.D.

Sahl bin Sa'ad. He was fifteen when the Prophet died. Among the companions of Medina he was the last to die.

Shaddad bin Aus. Nephew of the famous poet Hasan bin Sabet. A scholar in his own right who settled and died in Jerusalem.

Sha'wana. A great female mystic of Persia of the eighth century A.D. She lost her eyesight due to excessive tears of penance.

Sheikh Abdul Qadir Jillani. 1092–1183 A.D. One of the greatest sages ever. Born in the province of Jillan, Iran, he received his religious education in Baghdad. Given to austere discipline, he spent twenty five years worshiping alone in the woodlands of Iraq.

Shibli (Abu Bakr Dulaf bin Jahdar al-Shibli). A celebrated sheikh of the eleventh century A.D. He was the chief steward of the caliph but renounced his position once he was acquainted with the Truth.

Shu'aib bin Se'nam. An emancipated slave severely persecuted for embracing the new faith. One of the first to migrate to Medina. A companion of the Prophet.

Sufyan Thawri. An ascetic of the seventh century A.D. Given to austere discipline and much fasting, he renounced the world and wore coarse woolen cloth called Suf. Thus the term "Sufi."

Umar bin al-Khattab. Originally one of the fiercest opponents of the Prophet. Powerful and wealthy. His conversion to Islam gave the cause renewed vigor. The second caliph of the Islamic commonwealth after the death of the Prophet.

'Uqbah bin Amir. Belonged to the tribe of Sa'sa'ah. A companion of the Prophet.

Uthman bin Affan. Awakened one night with the voice "Sleepers awake! Ahmad has come to Mecca," he embraced the faith when Talha, a fellow Meccan, told him that a monk in Bostara had predicted the coming forth of Ahmad that month. A distant cousin of the Prophet, he was the third caliph of the Islamic commonwealth.

Wa'silah bin al-Asqa'a. Embraced Islam at the time of the campaign of Tabuk. An affluent merchant whose wealth helped the cause of Islam.

Notes

1. Short descriptions of those cited in the source lines can be found in the listing beginning on p. 387. Book references (e.g.: *Al-Hadis*) refer to the bibliography beginning on p. 383. The validity of the *hadith* (literally, "speech," "report," that is, the traditional accounts of things said or done by Muhammad or his companions) depends on the chain of transmission from the Prophet and his companions, thus the importance of the reporter of the tradition.

2. The Qur'an is divided into 114 chapters, called *surahs*. Each *surah* has a title, for example, "The Cow," "The Clans," "The Unbelievers," usually derived from a phrase in the *surah* but not necessarily describing the theme of the *surah* as a whole. So, for example, the title of *surah* 29, "The Spider," is taken from verse 41, which alludes to the infirmity of false beliefs; as frail as spider webs, they cannot withstand the onslaught of the winds of truth. The title "The Cow" is derived from the story narrated in 2:67–73, in which Moses asks his people to sacrifice a cow in the name of Allah; a long dialogue follows concerning the exact details pertaining to the sacrifice.

3. That is, the Ka'ba, the sacred mosque of Allah in Mecca, built by Abraham and Ishmael.

4. Qibla: The point toward which Muslims turn to pray, especially the Ka'ba, or House of God, at Mecca.

5. In Islamic belief, any of a class of spirits, lower than the angels, capable of appearing in both human and animal forms and influencing humankind for either good or evil.

6. Most of the Qur'an is written as the speech of God, who speaks in the first person plural ("We"). When Muhammad speaks to his listeners, his words are introduced by "Say," thus emphasizing that he is speaking at the bidding of Allah.

7. An allusion to the deception of life on earth. Through the light of their faith believers are delivered from falling into debauchery on earth and upon resurrection are saved from the doom of hellfire.

8. The Sabeans were a monotheistic religious group intermediate between Judaism and Christianity. They probably were followers of John the Baptist.

9. Mustafa: the divinely elected, one of the 201 attributes of Muhammad.

10. That is, the angels.

11. Dhikr: A congregation of people usually sitting in a circle, reciting the divine names of Allah, under the guidance of a sheikh. Allah has ninety-nine names and the foremost of these is Allah, the greatest name that includes all the other attributes.

12. In ancient times, and still in some parts of the Middle East, people wore soft leather, sock-like shoes. Though more convenient, slippers do not provide sanitary protection from the desert sands.

13. Jews and Christians.

14. See note 11 above.

15. The Israelites and the army of the Pharaoh when it caught up with them by the Red Sea.

16. Imam: Muslim religious leader.

17. Moses, who turned to God seeking forgiveness after he murdered an Egyptian oppressing a Hebrew.

18. See note 4 above.

19. 'Ali bin Abi Talib was called the Lion of God for his unrivaled valor and expertise in warfare.

20. The angels that record good and evil deeds.

21. Quresh: the tribe to which the Prophet belonged.

22. The people of Medina, who embraced Islam before the Meccans and received the Muslim refugees with open arms, sharing their homes with them although they were extremely poor themselves.

23. The Prophet Muhammad was called Ahmad (the praised one) before the revelation of the Qur'an.

24. The Prophet used to wrap himself in his cloak during his trances.

25. The Qur'an was revealed over a period of twenty-seven years.

26. The Prophet was in the middle of a conversation with one of the most influential chieftains of pagan Mecca, hoping to convert him to Islam and thereby persuading a large following. But he was interrupted by a blind man, Abdullah bin Shurah, who asked him to repeat a chapter of the Qur'an. The

Prophet "frowned at the blind man and turned his face away." There and then he was reproved by the above verse. In later years he often greeted Abdullah bin Shurah: "Welcome to him on whose account the Merciful rebuked me."

27. Reference to a barbaric pagan Arab custom of burying female offspring alive because they were considered superfluous.

28. The Night of Power: the awesome night when the first verse of the Lord's commandments was revealed, the night when all destinies are shaped, a night of peace when all evil is curtailed and the angels descend to earth with benediction.

29. Ka'ba: the sacred Mosque of Allah in Mecca, built by Abraham and Ishmael.

30. See note 4 above.